DIRT CHEAP

GARDENING

Hundreds of Ways to Save Money in Your Garden

Rhonda Massingham Hart

A Garden Way Publishing Book

Storey Communications, Inc.
Schoolhouse Road
Pownal, Vermont 05261

> The mission of Storey Communications is to serve our customers
> by publishing practical information that encourages personal independence
> in harmony with the environment.

Edited by Deborah L. Balmuth and Kirsten Halvorsen Stahl
Cover design by Greg Imhoff
Cover photograph by Cindy McFarland
Text design and production by Cindy McFarland and Susan Bernier
Line drawings by Brigita Fuhrmann
Indexed by Northwind Editorial Services

Garden Way Publishing was founded in 1973 as part of the Garden Way Incorporated Group of Companies, dedicated to bringing gardening information and equipment to as many people as possible. Today the name "Garden Way Publishing" is licensed to Storey Communications, Inc., in Pownal, Vermont. For a complete list of Garden Way Publishing titles call 1-800-827-8673. Garden Way Incorporated manufactures products in Troy, New York, under the Troy-Bilt® brand including garden tillers, chipper/shredders, mulching mowers, sicklebar mowers, and tractors. For information on any Garden Way Incorporated product, please call 1-800-345-4454.

Printed in the United States by R.R. Donnelley
First Printing, March 1995

Library of Congress Cataloging-in-Publication Data

Hart, Rhonda Massingham, 1959-
    Dirt-cheap gardening : hundreds of ways to save money in your garden / Rhonda Massingham Hart.
         p.   cm.
     "A Garden Way Publishing book."
     Includes bibliographical references (p.   ) and index.
     ISBN 0-88266-898-6
     1. Gardening. I. Title.
SB453.H327   1995
635—dc20   95-2173
                                  CIP

Dedication

To my father, Richard Massingham,
with love and gratitude.
Thanks, Dad.

Acknowledgements

I wish to express my gratitude to the Washington State University, Spokane County Extension Master Gardener's Program for much of the training and literature that made this book possible.

Special thanks to Nancy Cashon, the Plant Clinic Coordinator, for helping to nurse the book along in its infant stages and for putting up with all of my last-minute questions and double-checking.

My appreciation also goes to Scott McLaughlin of Country Homes Power Equipment in Spokane for his expertise on garden power equipment.

Finally, my heartfelt thanks to Chris Culbertson of Colby's Greenhouse for sharing his incredible knowledge, his honest opinions, and his limitless moral support during the writing of this book.

TABLE OF CONTENTS

THE DIRT ON CHEAP GARDENING

I've always been a little confused by all those books for lazy gardeners, because I don't know any. Gardeners seem compelled to work. Those green thumbs make our hands restless.

Many gardeners also have another characteristic in common; we like to save money. For some people, it leads them to grow their own food or mow their own lawns. Some people have to mow their lawns and grow gardens to survive, but for other people, it is merely a source of satisfaction.

Dirt-Cheap Gardening is for frugal people who garden. Filled with hundreds of tips on everything from acquiring seed and plants to harvesting your crops, this book can really help you garden inexpensively. But don't think for a minute that an inexpensive garden has to look cheap. If you expend a little time, energy, and creativity — without a lot of money — you will have a garden others envy.

Many of the tips also are time-saving ideas. Even though I am cheap, or frugal, I know nothing is more valuable than your time.

1
THE ABSOLUTES

What **elements** do you really **need** to start a garden? The simple requirements are soil, water and seed. But what about location of the soil, the *type* of soil, and its structure and content? How much water is necessary, and how will you deliver it? Thousands of seeds in garden varieties are available. How will you narrow your choices? Do you really want seeds, or should you get transplants instead? See what I mean, it's simple.

Let's begin with the first choice every budding gardener must make: the site of the garden. Whether you are landscaping a small, city plot or planting a large, country garden, you still must take stock of your site first.

Imagine what you'd do if you could choose the perfect garden site.

The Perfect Garden Site Avoids:

→ **Low-lying pockets.** Frost settles in low areas, air does not circulate freely.

→ **Exposed hilltops.** Exposure to wind and temperature extremes makes gardening a challenge.

→ **North-facing slopes.** They receive less sun and are often cooler than surrounding areas.

→ **Shade,** if planning a fruit or vegetable garden.

→ **Compacted ground,** such as former parking lots or areas where heavy machinery has been used. It's murder to convert such areas into decent growing soil.

→ **Subsoil.** Unfortunately, this describes almost all new housing sites — as well as parking lots, because contractors often scrape away precious topsoil.

→ **Sand or clay.** Both extremes have their challenges.

The Perfect Garden Site Features:

→ **A gentle south-facing slope.** It will receive full sun and the slope facilitates both water drainage and air circulation.

→ **Well-draining soil.** Test by digging a 1-foot-deep hole, and filling it with water. If it takes more than a few hours to drain, you may want to take steps to improve the drainage. (See "Soil Toil," page 9.)

→ **Fertile, friable loam,** rich in humus. Nobody ever just finds soil like this; it takes years of building. But it is nice to dream about it in a perfect site.

→ **Full sun.** Many plants prefer it, and you can surround those that require shade with trees, shrubs, or garden structures.

→ **Available water.** Realistically, how far are you willing to lug the garden hose?

Make the Most of Your Site by Finding Out About:

→ **The average rainfall** for your area.

→ **The average first and last frost dates,** from which you can then calculate your anticipated growing season.

→ **Low temperatures** in your area and your USDA Zone designation.

→ **Your soil's pH.** (See "Soil Toil," page 9.)

And Consider Such Facts As:

→ **Gardens in cities** are warmed by the artificial environment surrounding them, which extends the natural growing season. Plants and gardeners also must be able to tolerate air pollution.

→ **Seaside gardens** get whipped by salty winds, but are buffered from sudden temperature changes.

→ **Nearby bodies of water** substantially change the immediate growing conditions. They retain heat through the day and release it over a prolonged period of time.

→ **Higher elevations** usually mean lower temperatures.

The Right Site

Unfortunately, most of us don't get to choose the right garden site. We have a yard, and the garden goes there. Even the smallest yard, however, has a variety of growing areas within it, known as microclimates.

Exploit Microclimates

To understand microclimates a little better, let's look at a typical house and yard, as illustrated. The north side of the house is shady from mid-morning through the end of the day. The east side receives morning sun, but not direct sun in the afternoon. The south side's yard receives full sun all day long. And the west side of the house doesn't get full sun until mid-day,

MONEY-SAVING TIP
Put each plant in the most appropriate microclimate.

but then bakes until dusk. Each side of the house has a different set of growing conditions and is a distinct microclimate. Additional landscaping will create even more microclimates. A white painted fence along the yard, a pond, trees, and bushes will produce different growing conditions for plants near them.

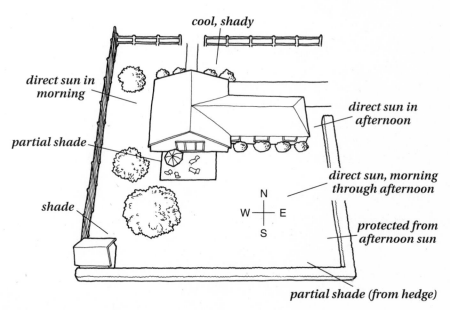

Look carefully at the microclimates surrounding your house so you can select plants that are best-suited to grow in each area.

Why should the cash-conscious gardener care about microclimates? Because if you plant things where they don't like to grow, it's a waste of money, time, and effort. Plants all have their own unique growing requirements. Some plants thrive in shade, while others falter there for lack of sunlight. When assessing your site, note your microclimates. They will help you decide what plants to grow and where to put them.

Work with Your Site

Refer to the list of things to look for in the perfect garden site on page 2. Does this sound like your yard? If you answered yes, congratulations; if not, consider some creative gardening tactics.

PLANTS THAT GROW BEST IN FULL SUN

ANNUALS/BIENNIALS	PERENNIALS	TREES/SHRUBS
Ageratum	Aster	Barberry
Sweet alyssum	Candytuft	Forsythia*
Calendula	Clematis	Fruit trees
Celosia	Columbine*	Junipers
Chamomile	Coralbells**	Mock orange
Cosmos	Coreopsis	Peony and tree
Garden vegetables	Creeping thyme	peony**
Lobelia	Crocus	Potentilla
Many herbs	Daffodils*	Russian olive
Marigold	Daisies*	Staghorn sumac
Moss rose	Daylily	White forsythia
Nasturtium	Blanket flower	
Petunia	Garden phlox	
Knotweed	Iris	
Salvia	Lady's mantle*	
Zinnia	Lilac	
	Ornamental grasses	
	Pinks	
	Purple coneflower	
	Roses	
	Rudbeckia	
	Sedum*	
	Sweet pea	
	Sunflower	
	Tulips	
	Violets*	
	Virginia creeper	
	Yarrow	
	Yucca	

* Tolerates some shade.
** Prefers partial shade in hot areas.

PLANTS THAT GROW BEST IN SHADE

ANNUALS/BIENNIALS	PERENNIALS	TREES/SHRUBS
Begonias	Astilbe*	Azalea
Foxglove	Bishop's weed	Blueberry
Impatiens	Bleeding heart	Fuchsia
	Bugleweed	Hydrangea
	Ferns, various	Oregon grape
	Garden phlox	Rhododendrons
	Hardy geranium	Viburnums
	Hosta	
	Pachysandra	
	Primroses	
	Vinca minor*	
	Viola	
	Yellow corydalis	

* Tolerates full sun in the north.

PLANTS THAT GROW BEST NEAR THE SEA

ANNUALS/BIENNIALS	PERENNIALS	TREES/SHRUBS
Blue cornflower	Blue fescue	Eucalyptus
Borage	Lantana	Norway maple
Calendula or pot	Lavender	Pine (several)
marigold	Sagebrush	Rugosa roses
Godetia	Sedum	Russian olive
Honesty	Southernwood	
Nasturtiums	Statice	
Pelargoniums	Tarragon	
Petunia	Wormwood	

PLANTS THAT ARE POLLUTION-RESISTANT

PERENNIALS		TREES/SHRUBS
Bergenia	Sedum	Austrian pine
Clematis	Trumpet vine	Bradford pear
Columbine	Virginia creeper	Flowering cherry
Grapes (some)		Flowering plum
Hosta		Gingko
Poplar		Magnolia
Climbing hydrangea		Maples
Iris		Willow
Rudbeckia		

PLANTS THAT GROW WELL IN WET SOIL

PERENNIALS	ANNUALS/BIENNIALS	TREES/SHRUBS
Astilbe	Sunflowers	Alder
Bergenia		Blueberry
Calla		Elderberry
Cattail		Pear
Daylilies		Red maple
Dichondra		Rose of Sharon
Iris		Willow
Mint		
Moss		
Primroses		
Skunk cabbage		

Chances are that your yard fulfills at least some of the specifications for the perfect garden site. Let's say it has adequate drainage, except for one corner; mostly full sun, again with exceptions; and available water. Take advantage of what you have. The areas with good drainage are great for fruit or vegetable gardening or perhaps a perennial or rose bed. They all do best in full sun, and they will require plenty of water. The boggy areas are not lost. As you read on you will discover a way to improve drainage without draining your pocketbook. But an easier solution is to work with the conditions you have. Willows and alder trees love having their roots wet. You also could choose smaller, moisture-loving plants such as primrose or Siberian iris. The shaded areas can harbor various ferns, hosta, astilbe, or annuals such as impatiens or begonias.

Plants that prefer specific types of sites will save you dollars, hours, and the endless frustration of trying to coax unfortunate plants into surviving in an unsuitable site. Some plants cost more than others. But keeping the wrong plants on life-support is much more expensive than choosing the most appropriate plant in the first place.

Consider Containers

What? Your garden site doesn't abide by *any* of the recommendations for a perfect site? Even if you are at the bottom of the north slope of a parking lot, you can still grow plants. The solution is to plant in containers.

Container growing is easy and can be cheap. The most important investment is not the container, but the growing medium.

Planting mixture. Almost any container will accommodate some

Mix Your Own Soil

A standard formula for mixing planting medium is:

> 1 part soil
> 1 part peat moss
> 1 part perlite, vermiculite *or* sharp, clean sand
> 1 part compost (optional)

Find a container large enough to suit your needs and stir in the above ingredients until thoroughly mixed.

type of plant. The biggest mistake gardeners make with containers is shoveling garden soil into them. It compacts when used in containers. Compacted soil squeezes out oxygen, dries out easily, and is difficult to wet again thoroughly. All this results in unhealthy plants. Even though dirt from your yard is free, to use it alone in containers will cost you.

There are countless reliable growing mediums sold in garden centers, and they are a good investment. But, you can mix your own for less money than you can buy it.

You can incorporate garden soil in your mix to save some money. Use only a rich, loamy soil and sift out any clods, stones, sticks, or other foreign matter. Healthy transplants and established plants can tolerate raw soil in the mix. If you are starting seeds, however, pasteurize the soil you add to your mix: Garden soil teems with tiny life-forms, from visible bugs to invisible ones. This is a dirty, smelly job and a great argument for germination mixes without soil. To kill off all soilborne organisms properly, heat soil to over 140°F for about thirty minutes. You can do this with pans in an oven.

Customize mixes for the type of plants you are growing. For plants requiring free drainage, such as cacti or succulents, add an extra part of sand or perlite. For those with specific nutritional requirements, mix in fertilizer accordingly.

The container. As for the containers you should use, there are a few things to consider. Will you be raising food or ornamentals in them? Never grow food crops in containers that have previously contained something unknown or questionable. Plant roots transport many toxins; they could end up on your dinner table. Also, the container must have drainage holes at the bottom. A larger container requires more and larger holes. Poor drainage kills off more plants than anything else.

The material the container is made of can affect the plants. Metal containers get very hot in direct sun and transmit the heat to tender plant roots. Black plastic pots absorb more heat than light-colored ones. But many plants, such as poinsettias, must have their roots in a dark environment. Wood containers may harbor fungi. Stone or brick containers absorb heat, and release it slowly. Terra cotta or clay pots are decorative, but they absorb water away from plant roots. Peat pots also absorb water from roots.

Lovely, decorative containers abound in trendy garden centers, and they can set you back a few bucks if you must have them. But creativity and an eye for unusual items are free.

Salvage an old pair of cowboy boots, and fill them to overflowing with lobelia or ivy geraniums. An old wheelbarrow makes a purposeful planter, deep enough for carrots, large enough for broccoli, and decorative enough for a variety of flowers and trailing vines. Wooden crates, dented metal buckets, plastic-lined wicker baskets, hollowed-out logs, leaky watering cans, antique milk cans, discarded lunch boxes, junked, claw-footed bathtubs, unseaworthy rowboats or canoes, and countless other finds make fun, functional, frugal planters. See what you can find.

Know Your Zone

The United States Department of Agriculture's cold hardiness zones, numbered from 1 to 11, indicate the average winter low temperatures to expect. This is crucial information, but it also can be misleading. It is

Create your own plant containers from found and recycled objects, large and small.

crucial, because if you live in zone 5 and buy plants listed as hardy to zone 8, they will die. The lower the zone number, the colder the expected winter lows. Plants that won't survive the lowest expected average, are a waste of money. But the zones's numbers can be misleading because we don't have many average winters.

When buying trees, shrubs, or perennials, always select varieties listed as cold hardy to your area. Better yet, opt for those that can withstand the next coldest zone. So when a colder than average winter occurs, your carefully spent plant dollars will not be wasted.

 USDA Plant Hardiness Zones

Zone 1: Temperature drops below -50°F (-46°C)
Zone 2: Lows from   -50°   to   -40°F   (-46° to -40°C)
Zone 3: Lows from   -40°   to   -30°F   (-40° to -34°C)
Zone 4: Lows from   -30°   to   -20°F   (-34° to -29°C)
Zone 5: Lows from   -20°   to   -10°F   (-29° to -23°C)
Zone 6: Lows from   -10°   to   0°F   (-23° to -18°C)
Zone 7: Lows from   0°   to   10°F   (-18° to -12°C)
Zone 8: Lows from   10°   to   20°F   (-12°C to -7°C)
Zone 9: Lows from   20°   to   30°F   (-7° to -1°C)
Zone 10: Lows from   30°   to   40°F   (-1° to 4°C)
Zone 11: Lows above 40°F   (Above 4°C)

Soil Toil

Thou shalt not skimp on soil preparation! The more you put into your soil, the more you will get out of it. What, you may ask, is the big deal? Dirt is still dirt, right? The truth is your soil health predicts the health of your entire garden. Rich, healthy soil sustains healthy plants that are more productive and give you the best possible return for your gardening investment. They also cost little or nothing in pesticides, fertilizers, and replacement.

MONEY-SAVING TIP
Start with healthy soil for healthier, longer-lived plants.

Cultivate a Sense of Humus

For a better understanding, look at the functions of soil in your garden. Soil provides physical support for the plants and a reservoir for nutrients, water, and oxygen. Some soils do the second part better than others. Sandy soils drain quickly, providing plenty of oxygen, but they also lose water, and dissolve nutrients too quickly. Clay holds minerals and moisture well, but drains poorly. The magic ingredient for improving either type of soil, or any type in between, is humus.

Humus is organic matter that has gone through a degrading experience. Organic matter is the remains of previously living things, such as plants, micro-organisms, bugs, and us. When added to sandy soils, humus improves water retention by attracting water molecules. When added to clay, humus improves drainage by breaking up the clay particles that naturally cling together. Humus also provides fuel for millions of micro-organisms that reside in the soil. As they break it down, the micro-organisms release elements necessary for plant growth.

High levels of humus are a sign of well-managed soil. It is best to add small amounts of humus each year and build it up, rather than dump it all on in one application. This is important because in the process of decaying organic matter, micro-organisms tie up precious soil nitrogen, which must be replenished. A good rule of thumb is to add not more than 4 inches of organic matter each year to any garden area.

Incorporating humus into your garden can be as cheap or expensive as you make it. Not surprisingly, the cheaper ways are more work than the expensive ones. The ideal way to incorporate humus is to compost. (See pages 93–97 about compost piles.) Barnyard manures also provide plenty of partially processed organic matter. Of course, garden centers offer bags of dried organic matter in the form of peat moss, processed compost, and steer manure. The advantage of compost, manures, or commercial products containing fertilizers is they also contain soil nutrients, usually including necessary nitrogen. So while it is less expensive to compost your own, the good news about buying bags of fertilizer is your money will be well-spent.

Is Your Soil Nutritious?

So you agree humus is good stuff. But will your soil contain all the nutrients necessary for healthy plant growth if all you add to it is humus? You already know incorporating organic matter that becomes humus means you will probably have to add nitrogen. Plants also need many other nutrients.

With the exception of carbon, which plants take from carbon dioxide in the air, as well as hydrogen and oxygen, which they derive from water, all other elements plants use must come directly from the soil. So what do they need?

The major elements are those listed on plant food labels as N (nitrogen), P (phosphorus), and K (potassium, available as potash or K_2O). Many soils are naturally high or low in any of these, but nitrogen is the most water soluble, and therefore the most likely to leach away (and into ground-water supplies). Adding more nitrogen than plants can take up is a waste of money.

MONEY-SAVING TIP
Don't waste money giving plants more nutrient supplements than they can absorb.

The elements plants use less of are called secondary elements. They are no less critical to healthy growth than the major elements; plants just require smaller doses of them. They are calcium (Ca), magnesium (Mg), and sulfur (S). Don't waste money by adding these to your soil on a yearly basis, because plants take them in slowly, and they don't leach away. A single application usually lasts several years.

Trace or micronutrients are those that plants require only small amounts of. They include boron (B), manganese (Mn), copper (Cu), zinc (Zn), iron (Fe), molybdenum (Mo), and chlorine (Cl). Short of a soil test, the best way to tell if you need to add any of these is by plant response.

Where to Get Cheap Soil Amendments

You know you want humus or organic matter and also that other nutrients are necessary for soil and plant health. But before you run down to the garden center, let's consider some alternative low-cost soil

 Tomatoes Tell All

Here's a reason to grow tomatoes even if you don't like them. They are sensitive to soil abnormalities and show distinct symptoms in cases of soil deficiencies. For instance, the youngest leaves of tomatoes grown in iron-deficient soils turn yellow between the veins, with the base of the leaflets showing the most discoloration. The youngest leaves on tomato plants grown in calcium-poor soils turn purplish-brown. You can grow tomato plants for their diagnostic skills.

amendments, where you can get them, and how they will help your garden.

Compost. Your own backyard is the best and cheapest place to find this valuable soil amendment (see pages 93–97 for how to make your own). You also will find it in the garden center's soil amendment section. Also, cities and counties are getting into the act with community composting. You can find huge heaps of the stuff near your local trash dump. Bring your own containers or a pick-up truck, and get your share for nothing or a nominal fee.

Mushroom compost. If you happen to live near a mushroom grower, they are an excellent source for low-cost or free compost. Mushrooms are grown indoors in huge containers filled with fine, dark, crumbly compost. Before growers plant mushroom spawn in containers, they steam-sterilize the compost. After a couple of months, growers harvest the mushrooms and clear out the bins. This used compost is still rich in nutrients and organic matter. A few little mushrooms may pop up, but since you know they are an edible variety, eat up.

Sewage sludge. Plants treat sewage for disposal using two methods, anaerobic digestion and air activation. Digested sludge is much lower quality as a fertilizer than the activated type. Activated sludge is usually much more expensive. Either type of heat-treated sludge is safe to use around your yard and garden. Inquire at your local treatment plant.

Green manures. When you spade green vegetation into the soil, you add precious organic matter, nutrients, and moisture. Green leaves, weeds, grass clippings, and cover crops such as clovers, buckwheat, rye, and oats return nitrogen, carbon, trace minerals, and other nutrients to the soil when turned under. Legumes, such as clover and alfalfa, make exceptional cover crops because they take nitrogen from the air, and convert it into a usable form for plants. One word of caution: If your plants go to seed, don't turn them into your garden soil — unless you want more of them.

Animal manures. Where there are animals, there will be manure. The first rule is never use cat, dog, or swine manure in your garden. These types of manure harbor parasites and disease organisms that can be harmful to your health.

Racetracks, livestock breeding farms, dairy farms, rabbit runs, poultry farms, petting zoos, and non-petting zoos often are overjoyed to have someone actually volunteer to haul the manure away! Most manures should not be used fresh in the garden; salts will burn plant roots. Compost it first, or spread it over the soil in the fall so it has time to mellow.

Rendering plants. Organic gardeners are familiar with additives such as blood meal (rich in nitrogen), hoof and horn meal (high in nitrogen, phosphorus, and calcium), and bone meal (rich in nitrogen, phosphorus, and calcium). These are by-products of the slaughtering process and originate at rendering plants. Purchased in small quantities, these products are usually quite expensive. Most rendering plants sell these only in bulk, such as 25-ton tractor/trailer loads. Make friends with a plant worker who may be able to get you a smaller quantity!

Restaurants. Coffee grounds from espresso bars or coffee brewers are a good source of nitrogen. Ask the brewer to empty coffee grounds into a container for you to pick up once a week. The grounds are fairly acidic and useful in lowering pH levels when heavily applied.

Lumber mills. Sawdust is the by-product of turning trees into boards. Composed of cellulose, sawdust is a good form of organic matter for your garden. Don't add more than 2 inches each year as it requires a lot of nitrogen to decompose. For each ton of sawdust, a garden burns about 3½ pounds of pure nitrogen. Offset this by adding 17 pounds of ammonium sulfate, 11 pounds of ammonium nitrate, **or** 8 pounds of urea. Avoid cedar sawdust, because it is toxic to some seedlings. Alderwood dust decomposes more quickly than others, such as fir or hemlock.

pH Simplified

Acidity and alkalinity describe measurements of the pH balance. The pH level is measured on a scale from 1 to 14. 1 is extremely acidic, 14 extremely alkaline, and 7 is neutral. Each number represents a tenfold difference in acidity or alkalinity. Soil that has a pH of 6 is ten times more acidic than soil with a pH of 7. Most plants prefer a slightly acidic soil, while some, such as blueberries, prosper only in very acidic soils. Very high or very low pH affects the availability of soil elements to plants, which makes pH a key factor in nutrient supply.

Gardeners commonly alter pH with lime and sulfur products. Lime raises pH (reduces acidity) and sulfur lowers pH (raises acidity). Since young plants are very sensitive to pH levels, add amendments the season *before* you plant to give the additive time to change the acid balance. Often gardeners are impatient and don't give purchased products a fair chance to work, simply another waste of money. Also, apply lime at least thirty days prior to using fertilizers; they bind each other up when applied together, essentially wasting the money spent on both products.

Other soil additives also affect pH balance. When applied heavily,

MONEY-SAVING TIP
Use soil amendments effectively by applying them in appropriate order and allowing time for each to work before applying more.

manures, sludge, peat moss, coffee grounds, and high-nitrogen fertilizers raise acidity.

A Simple Test

There are three kinds of soil tests. One you buy at the garden center that lets you play with test tubes and litmus paper. Professional labs perform another type of test. The lab sends back coded messages that James Bond 007 couldn't decipher and a big bill to boot. You perform the third type of test by paying attention to your plants.

If your soil lacks any given nutrient that affects your plants, they will tell you. Nitrogen deficiencies are among the most common. Plants, especially tomatoes, respond with slow growth and yellowing foliage. Other deficiencies produce their own side effects.

PLANTS THAT PREFER ACID SOIL

SLIGHTLY ACIDIC	MODERATELY ACIDIC	VERY ACIDIC
Aster	Aster	Rhododendron
Cosmos	Heather	Azalea
Marigolds	Herald's trumpet	Barberry
Pansies	Trillium	Blueberry
Phlox		Camelia
Snapdragons		Dogwoods
Zinnias		Heath
		Hydrangea

PLANTS THAT PREFER ALKALINE SOIL

SLIGHTLY ALKALINE	MODERATELY ALKALINE	VERY ALKALINE
Ageratum	Baby's breath	Box
Cosmos	Bergenia	Cotoneaster
Marigold	Corydalis	Euonymus
Snapdragon	Fernleaf yarrow	Forsythia
Sweet alyssum	Peonies	Lilac
		Mock orange
		Potentilla
		Rugosa rose

The final argument against splurging on soil tests is even if they do tell you what you have in your soil, they don't often tell you what to do about it. If you really feel you need to test your soil, contact your Cooperative Extension Service for advice pertinent to your area.

There are times when a soil test is useful. If you are actually at a point where your plants are not performing well, by all means run a test. If you have just built a new home on sub-soil battered by heavy machinery, that is justification. If you wish to grow acid-loving plants, such as blueberries, get an inexpensive pH meter and test routinely.

Water Wisdom

How you deliver water to your plants will have a major impact on your watering costs. If you are on a community water supply, you can cut

CONTENTS OF SOIL AMENDMENTS

Source	Percent Nitrogen	Percent Phosphorus	Percent Potassium	pH
Blood meal	12 to 15	1.2	1	
Bone meal	2 to 4	15 to 25		
Coffee grounds	2	.3	.7	4.5
Compost	1 to 3	1	1	
Cow (Dairy)	.5 to 2	.2 to .3	.5 to 1	
Feathers	12 to 15	0	0	
Hoof/horn meal	6 to 15	2	0	
Horse manure	.6 to .8	.4	.4	
Llama manure	1 to 2	.4	.4	
Poultry manure	2 to 4	1 to 3.5	.4 to 2	
Activated sludge	5 to 6	3 to 7	1 or less	4.5 to 5.5
Digested sludge	1 to 3	.5 to 4	.5 or less	5.5 to 7.0
Steer (Feeder)	.8 to 1	.3 to .4	.4	
Zoo manure	.8 to 1.2	.4 to .6	.5	

your monthly bill significantly with wily watering. If you water from a well, you will save on the cost of running a pump. Either way you will conserve water.

While in the past, we merely turned on the sprinkler and walked away, today water conservation is a top priority. Water bills are not the only reason. Drought and heavy demand call for careful management of this most precious resource.

Are You All Wet?

If you still use a lawn sprinkler to water a vegetable garden or landscape planting, or if you use an overhead watering system on hot, windy days you are wasting water. The idea of watering is to deliver an adequate amount of water to plant roots, no more, no less, and nowhere else.

There are several factors that determine how much water you need to apply and the best method of application. For starters, rainfall is a factor. No matter what plants you are watering in what type of soil, the amount of watering necessary depends on how much nature already supplies.

Another factor is the soil type. Remember that sandy soils drain quickly and that clay holds moisture for a longer period of time. These are functions of how the water moves through the soil, which affects its availability to plant roots. One inch of water applied in sandy soil will percolate down 12 inches. In good loam 1 inch of water will go down 6 to 10 inches, and in clay it will penetrate about 4 or 5 inches. Once water has filtered down beneath plant root zones it is effectively gone.

Finally, consider the plants you are watering. Some plants need much more water than others. New plants, from seeded lawns to bedding transplants and burlap-balled shrubs, require lots of frequent watering to establish their roots. On the other hand, established native plants need very little rainfall supplementation; they have naturally adapted to the area. Some plants, such as madrona, flannel bush, and western dogwood, suffer if watered in the summer.

How Much Is Just Right?

MONEY-SAVING TIP
Avoid using inappropriate watering systems such as lawn sprinklers for vegetable gardens.

While there is no one answer to the question of how much water is just right for all gardens, there are some useful general guidelines. The most efficient and cost-effective way to water any plant is to fill the entire root zone with water, and let the soil become almost dry before the next watering. The amount of dryness depends on the plant. Let the top 2 or 3 inches dry out for most established plants. Let the soil around a large tree dry down several inches, but keep new or tiny plants moist to the top inch or so of soil.

MONEY-SAVING TIP
If water is scarce or expensive in your area, choose plants that require less water.

Water most plants deeply and infrequently. When using a sprinkler, measure how many inches of water you apply by setting jars at intervals along sprinkler pathways. This will also tell you if the sprinkler gives even coverage.

Remember soil type affects how much water is necessary. Water sandy soils more frequently than clay soil. To make sure you are delivering enough water to where it is needed, use a soil probe or shovel before you water to determine the extent of dryness. Repeat the process after watering to see how deeply the water has penetrated into the soil.

Lawns. Use an overhead sprinkler. Water to a depth of at least 6 inches as soon as grass fails to spring up after walking on it. Avoid frequent, shallow waterings as they lead to shallow roots, which are far more susceptible to heat or drought. Aeration, or removal of soil plugs, helps send water to the root zone. Renting an aerator every other year or so also will help to reduce thatch build-up and combat compaction.

Vegetables, Bedding Plants, and Perennials. Water 6 to 12 inches deep every four to ten days for established plants. Don't wait for plants to wilt before the next watering. Wilting slows growth and reduces crop yields.

Soaker hoses or drip irrigation are efficient ways to water here (see Chapter 2). They can save up to 60 percent of the water used by a sprinkler. Place mulch (see Chapter 7) over the hose to prevent evaporation.

A cheap version of drip irrigation is container watering. Bury a container, such as a plastic 1-gallon milk jug that has had 2 or 3 holes punched in the bottom, next to or between individual plants. Keep the containers filled with water and allow them to seep water directly into plant root zones. Tailor the size of the container to the size of the plant.

Sprinklers are not the best for vegetable gardens because they waste a vast amount of water. More water lands on the leaves, where it evaporates, than anywhere else. Hand watering is as much a waste of time as it is water. Unless you stand there for a few **hours** with a water wand, you cannot wet the soil deeply enough to do a worthwhile job.

Cultivate unmulched soil to increase water absorption. Crusted soil

forms a barrier against water penetration.

Trees, Shrubs, and Landscape Plants. Water throughout the drip line of plants for the most efficient intake of water. Soaker hoses (see page 31) allow you to wind around individual plants. They are great for such shrubs as roses that are susceptible to moisture-loving disease organisms. Since no water rests on the leaves the diseases can't establish their spores. To allow water to slowly seep down into the soil, mound a ridge of soil around the outside of the drip line to form a basin and fill with water. Remove this soil during rainy weather to prevent waterlogged roots.

Plants on landscape berms. Check and water more frequently since they have more exposed soil from which water may evaporate.

New woody transplants. Water thoroughly both the nursery soil within the root ball and the native soil surrounding it. Failure to do so may prevent the roots from venturing into the surrounding soil, which can eventually kill the plant. Dead plants are an investment wasted.

Plants in containers. Water as soon as the surface feels dry. Keep a close eye on thirsty plants such as fuschias, which often need watering once or twice *daily* in hot, dry weather.

Water Loss Means We All Lose

In a perfect world every drop of water you put on your plants would run straight to the roots and would be used immediately by the plant. But we have to deal with water loss. Knowing how to reduce it saves water and money.

Moisture is lost from the soil in several ways, but you can cut these losses. By incorporating lots of humus into the soil, you will lessen the amount of water that percolates through the soil and out of reach. Humus is a water magnet. A lot of water is also lost through evaporation from the soil surface. Thanks to capillary action through the soil, which draws water up from below, evaporation can deplete water from deep in the ground. Keeping the soil surface covered with mulch (see pages 109–111) protects against this. Another line of defense against evaporation is to get less of the soil surface wet in the first place. This means replacing a sprinkler with a drip system, soaker hose, or individual water containers for landscape or large vegetable plants. Finally, transpiration, the way in which plants metabolize water, can steal amazing quantities of water from your soil. One large shade tree on a hot sum-

Mounding the soil around the dripline of a shrub helps retain water.

You can set up a rainbarrel equipped with spigot and drip tubing to make your own cheap gravity-flow irrigation system.

mer day can transpire several *hundred* gallons of water. Misting plants on hot, dry days helps limit the amount transpired and reduces plant stress.

As mentioned, air evaporation is also a major water waster if you use an overhead sprinkler. Water early in the morning or at night for the least water loss. If you want to keep your water bill down, never water during hot, windy weather.

Save Through Planning

Most of us have more water than we know what to do with. Even in arid regions there are occasional deluges of rain. Rainbarrels are not a

MONEY-SAVING TIP
Group plants
together that need
heavier watering so
you can concentrate
the water in just a
few locations.

new idea, but still a useful one. Position clean, empty barrels beneath downspouts or up on blocks around the garden. Barrels, positioned a few inches above the ground, can incorporate spigots and drip tubing for a cheap, gravity-flow irrigation system. A barrel positioned high above the ground creates strong water pressure, and far-flowing water. This time-honored method is excellent for flower or vegetable gardens.

Lawns are water hogs. They also consume their share of fertilizer, mowing time, and expense. Compared to native landscaping or a xeriscaped yard they are a ludicrous luxury. (Xeriscaping is the landscaping art of combining drought-tolerant plants, garden design, and water-conserving tactics to create a low-maintenance landscape.)

Consider reducing water and other bills by creating a smaller lawn. You may even find that by enlisting the services of a *paid* professional landscaper, you could save buckets of money. Or try gradually replacing some of the grass with less thirsty landscape plants. (See next page and pages 65–66 for examples.)

Be aware of which plants require the most water. Group them together so you don't waste water on plants that don't need it. Plants such as rhododendrons, azaleas, and ferns need more water than cacti. Also, if your yard has a naturally moist microclimate, put the water hogs there, not on the driest point of the property. Consider landscape points of interest that doesn't require water, such as a dry creek-bed of rock. Make it appear wet by varnishing the rocks. Position sprinklers to avoid watering sidewalks, streets, decks, and other structures; they won't grow.

Pennywise Plants

It is impossible to overemphasize the importance of choosing plants carefully. Some plants just give you more for the money.

While Chapter 4 goes into details about specific recommended plants and varieties, there are some basic truths to share here. One is that the most expensive plants are not necessarily the best. They may be rare, new, or the result of years of research and plant breeding, but none of that ensures they are best for your garden.

Is Bigger Better?

There are many things to consider before spending your hard-earned dollars at the nursery. With landscaping especially, the size of the plants you buy determines your immediate results. But it is their size at maturity that determines how your yard will *eventually* look. Younger plants are cheaper, but take longer to fulfill your dreams of a perfect yard, unless they grow fast. The downside to quick-growing plants is they often have a short life span. The pennywise answer is combine "fast-growers" to give you something to show for your money right away, with "long-livers" to sustain your investment.

FAST-GROWING VS. LONG-LIVED PLANTS

Key: GC: Ground Cover; P: Perennial: Sh: Shrub; T: Tree; V: Vine

Fast-Growing Plants

Bugleweed GC
Acacia T
Black-eyed susan vine V
Butterfly bush Sh
Cistus Sh
Eucalyptus T
Flowering plum T
Fuchsia Sh
Hazelnut T
Hibiscus Sh
Hydrangea Sh
Lantana Sh, V
Maples T
Ornamental grasses GC
Pine T
Poplar T
Quaking aspen T
Roses Sh, V
Sweet peas V
Weigela florida Sh
Willow T

Long-Lived Plants

Barberries Sh
Burning bush Sh
Conifers T
Daylilies* P
Flowering quince Sh
Forsythia Sh
Ginkgo T
Grapes V
Hawthornes Sh/T
Lilac Sh/T
Maples T
Rhubarb P
Roses (old garden, ramblers) Sh, V
Wisteria V

* Clumps, not necessarily the original plants, last indefinitely.

Longer Life Stretches Your Dollar

The longer a plant lives, the more you will get for your money. Food plants yield more crops over a longer period of time. Flowers, whether for cutting or bedding, bloom longer. Several factors limit longevity, however, not the least of which is genetics.

MONEY-SAVING TIP
Invest in longer-living plants and perennials that will come back year after year.

Like us, plants have a somewhat predetermined life-span. The entire life-cycle of annuals lasts a single season. Perennials come back every year. Though annuals are cheaper than perennials, you must replace them every year. A dollar spent on a six-pack of petunias may seem like a bargain compared to three dollars for a single candytuft, until you multiply the cost over several years. You only pay for perennials once.

2

TOOLS VS. TOYS

Efficient, cost-effective gardening requires some tools, but certain gadgets are not all they're cracked up to be. Knowing which tools are appropriate for which jobs will help you tell tools from toys.

A Tool for Every Task

Ancient ruins reveal crude gardening instruments in the form of sticks with metal blades attached. Humans used clay urns to carry water. That was about it; there were no rototillers or riding lawn mowers. Yet somehow the human race evolved from hunter-gatherers to farmers.

MONEY-SAVING TIP
Buy a new tool only
if it does the job
better than the one
you already have.

If a few crude tools were enough to transform humanity, they are enough to get you by in the garden. Whether you opt for more sophisticated, expensive hardware depends on your priorities. If you really want to save money in the garden, only buy a tool if it does the job better than what you are using. Make sure you buy the best-quality tools you can afford. Well-made tools last longer and require fewer repairs. Those necessary repairs are always cheaper than buying new tools. Also, consider versatility when buying tools. The more one tool can do for you, the fewer tools you will need.

People-Powered or Hand Tools

These are the fundamental tools necessary for gardening. They do not contribute to air or noise pollution, cost virtually nothing to operate, and require little cleaning and maintenance. Yet with a little people-power, these tools perform any task in the garden.

Cultivating tools primarily move around soil. They have a metal head and wooden, metal, or plastic handle. Look for carbon steel or stainless steel heads. If kept clean and dry between uses, carbon steel should not rust. Stainless steel is more expensive, but is rust-proof and makes work easier as soil falls away from it. Coatings on blades can wear off over time, making them a questionable expenditure. Wooden handles, such as hickory, are generally strong, and unlike metal or plastic, can be replaced if broken. Buy a handle that is of a comfortable length for you to use.

Forks loosen soil, cultivate, move bulky materials, such as weed piles and manure, and they lift root crops. In short, forks are versatile. Most forks have four, sturdy, metal prongs attached to a wooden or metal shaft. The best quality forks are those with the prongs and neck forged from a single piece of metal. Avoid forks pieced together or welded. Short-handled hand forks lift up plants and work well for knee-level weeding.

Hoes cultivate, weed, and form seed rows. They may have long or short handles with a blade attached. There are several types of hoes with specific uses. A Dutch hoe or scuffle hoe works well to remove small,

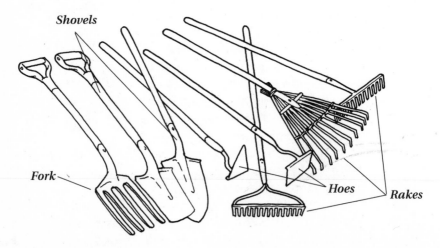

It's worth investing in the fundamental gardening tools: forks, hoes, rakes, spades, shovels, and trowels.

surface weeds around plants. A combination hoe has prongs on one side for breaking up soil and a blade on the other for chopping or moving around soil. A triangular hoe creates V-shaped furrows. Hand hoes have short handles and small, narrow blades for cultivating between closely spaced plants.

Rakes create an even and level soil surface as well as rake debris. A forged metal, toothed head, attached to a wooden or metal handle, pulls material. Those with the most teeth work the fastest, because they cover more ground each time you rake. Flathead rakes last longer than bow-head types. Lawn rakes compared to cultivating rakes, are lightweight, and have flexible tines designed to move light debris such as leaves or mown grass.

Spades and shovels dig and turn soil. Splurge on a stainless steel one if you can, as it takes a lot of strain out of digging. A rounded spade turns over soil, while a pointed shovel digs into the ground as well.

Trowels are mini-shovels, great for digging small transplanting holes. They are especially handy for working in containers.

Other cultivating tools include pronged and tooth-wheeled models. The prongs or teeth break up the soil, but work well only after the soil has already been cultivated, and only to a shallow depth.

Pruning tools cut woody growth. Pruning is necessary to keep many plants in their prime (See Chapter 7). Short- or long-handled pruners, saws, and knives are examples of hand-held pruning tools.

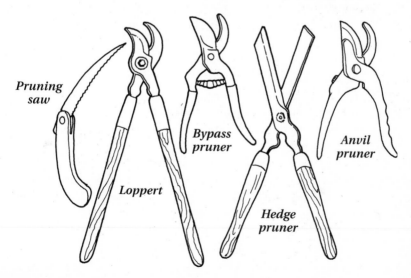

Pruning saw

Bypass pruner

Anvil pruner

Loppert

Hedge pruner

High-quality pruners with stainless- or carbon-steel blades are worth the investment. Their clean, crisp cuts help prevent plant infection.

Pruners work like scissors to snip branches. Buy pruners that give a clean, crisp cut. Ragged edges can leave plants open to infection. Get the best-quality stainless- or carbon-steel blade you can afford. Bypass pruners are the most versatile. Anvil pruners, unless kept *very* sharp, crush stems. Coated grips are worth the expense; they are more comfortable to use than bare steel.

Loppers are long-handled pruners used to cut branches in hard-to-reach places. The leverage created by the long handles makes cutting small branches a snap, and the shears can handle limbs 2 inches thick or more.

Tree pruners cut high branches. They work on a lever system, and some models can extend your reach up to 15 feet high. For most jobs though, a ladder and loppers will suffice.

Saws prune heavy branches. Of the several types available, a Grecian saw is one of the most versatile. It has a curved handle and teeth designed to cut only as you pull towards youself, making it easier to use in tight spaces. Bow saws work quickly, but are unwieldy to use in close quarters.

Knives have many uses in the garden. Use them for pruning, taking cuttings, grafting, and harvesting. A good pocket knife with a sharp, carbon-steel blade is a fine investment.

Shears can trim hedges, snip grass, cut back perennials, or create topiary masterpieces. Look for those with straight, sharp blades on sturdy wooden handles.

Lawn-care tools control where and how your grass grows.

Edgers make a clean cut at the border where grass meets another ground cover, such as pavement or planting beds. A sharp, half-moon-shaped head slices away sod. A sharp spade or garden knife does the same job.

Hand-held weeders such as ball weeders or a notched asparagus knife are useful for popping weeds out of the lawn without tearing up the turf.

Push-reel mowers may be a relic whose time has returned. Rotating blades cut grass evenly and provide a workout at the same time. Compared to motorized models, they are cheap to purchase, and they don't have any operating costs, except for occasionally sharpening the blades. Push-reel mowers also don't emit pollutants from burning fuel.

Spreaders apply fertilizer to lawns. There is a shoulder-carried version in which you turn a crank to spin granules out onto the lawn. But the more useful option is a hopper on wheels that you push. Most let you adjust the rate of application to your needs.

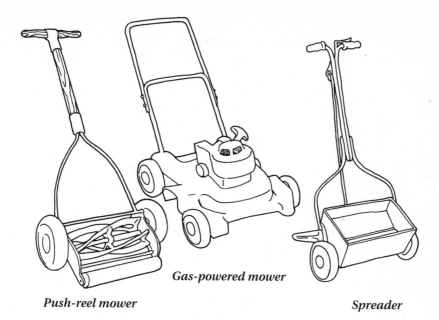

Gas-powered mower

Push-reel mower   *Spreader*

Gas- and Electric-Powered Tools

Most power tools constitute a hefty initial investment, which must be worked off over a period of time. They also represent a monetary commitment to run; they require fuel or electricity, maintenance, and, occasionally, repairs. The trade-off is they save time and effort.

Chipper/shredders reduce garden waste by three-quarters or more. They can be a real boon if you are clearing brush, especially if you cannot burn. Chippers and shredders chop branches, twigs, and leaves into a homogenous mix which can be used as mulch. Shredders also can speed up the process of composting (See Chapter 6). Since the heavy-duty branch-eaters also make short work of leaves, they are the most versatile. Gas-powered models are the fastest and noisiest. Both types can be dangerous.

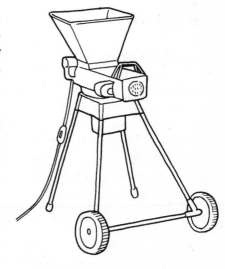

Chipper

Rototillers cultivate soil. Models range from 1 horsepower, lightweight tiller/cultivators, designed mainly for mechanized weeding, to 14 horsepower tillers, made for breaking new ground. Sharp digging tines rotate and cultivate the soil to depths varying from 4 to 8 inches. Considering that most plant roots penetrate at least 1 foot deep, a rototiller alone cannot prepare the soil deeply enough to accommodate them. The digging tines may be mounted in the front or rear of the machine. Except for the most powerful models, those de-signed with rear-mounted tines can be difficult to control at tilling depths greater than 3 inches. Rototillers can be

Rototiller

dangerous; never buy one without a deadman control. This safety feature stops the machine and the turning tines when engaged.

Lawn mowers cut grass. It's that simple. You may push, follow a self-propelled mower, or ride in style, but you are still simply cutting grass. The only real difference in cutting grass is how much you sweat, and whether the clippings are dropped, bagged, or mulched. Mulching mowers grind the clippings into tiny pieces that work their way back to the soil level. The tiny clippings provide beneficial mulch and eliminate waste. Self-propelled mowers generally cost at least $100 more than similar push-powered models, and the self-propelled models are twice as likely to need repairs. If your yard is small and level, you can get by with the less expensive push mower. If you have hills or a lot of ground to cover the self-propelled model may be better for you.

Some lawn-mower models have a blade-brake-clutch safety system which allows you to disengage the blade action without shutting down the engine. This is a real plus for moving the machine around when it's not actually cutting, say from the garage to the yard. Another helpful feature is a rear-bagging model, as opposed to a side-bagging one; they tend to be more maneuverable. Rear-wheel-drive machines, not front-wheel-drive models, have better traction. If you have physical limitations or a huge lot, a riding mower or lawn tractor may be necessary. Lawn tractors cost more but have the advantage of various accessories from garden carts to snow blades. They are also slightly less prone to repair jobs than riding mowers. Most lawn tractors can't rival the

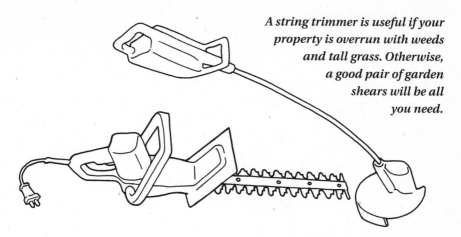

A string trimmer is useful if your property is overrun with weeds and tall grass. Otherwise, a good pair of garden shears will be all you need.

Electric hedge trimmers are cheaper and more lightweight than gas-powered models.

carpetlike evenness walk-behind mowers leave, and expect to spend more money. Don't even consider a lawn tractor without a deadman control in the seat. With the control, as soon as the driver leaves the seat, the engine stops. *Tip:* Lawn mowers go on sale after the Fourth of July.

String trimmers cut unruly herbaceous growth from weeds to overgrown grass. There are gas- and electric-powered models, but unless you have enough weeds to warrant the gas type, a good pair of garden shears will work instead. Some trimmers can also edge lawns; turn them so the string spins vertically.

Hedge trimmers are for yards with lots of big hedges. Gas-powered models are easy to use, cordless, and have little vibration. But they are loud and expensive. Electric trimmers are cheaper and more lightweight. Those with reciprocating blades, two blades cutting against each other are the most efficient. For most uses, a 16-inch blade is sufficient.

Leaf blowers move leaves. In a large area, a blower will save effort and time over a rake. There are hand-carried, back-pack, and push types, some with attachments. They are loud and expensive, and they take all the fun out of raking leaves.

Water Works

Watering equipment can be costly, but it may save you in the long run by lowering your water bills or pumping costs.

Water containers are for carrying and dispensing water. Stores sell all kinds of expensive watering cans, but you can make cheap imitations. Plastic milk or water jugs are ideal. Punch holes in the bottom, put on the cap, and carry upside-down. Turn them over, and remove the cap to sprinkle water.

Garden hoses carry water from a faucet to its final destination. They vary in length and can be screwed together to cover long distances. Water pressure from the source forces water through the hose to the end. Rubber and vinyl hoses are the most common, and are available in ½-inch, ⅝-inch, ¾-inch, and 1-inch diameters. Rubber lasts the longest and is least prone to kinking and splitting. For most uses a ⅝-inch size is the best buy. Look for hoses with a lifetime guarantee. Hoses go on sale in spring and fall.

Lawn sprinklers attach to a hose and spray water up and out. They are a tremendous improvement over hand watering for the time they save. Water pressure propels the spray in one of several patterns, with some types covering a larger area than others. The cheapest sprinklers cost between $5 and $8 and are small heads with holes punched in them. They rest on the ground and shoot water up over a limited area. These work all right for lawns, but in a border or vegetable garden the spray may be blocked by foliage. Rotating and pulse-jet sprinklers have moving parts that deliver an even spray. Impulse-jet types are the most versatile, because you can adjust them to water a range of patterns, including a full circle. Oscillating sprinklers have a rocking bar that sprays water. They are not the best for vegetable plots, flower borders, or landscaping plants, because so much water lands on foliage instead of near the roots. If you must use a sprinkler in these spots, elevate it with a step-ladder or other substitute so the spray lands unobstructed. Look for sales in spring and fall.

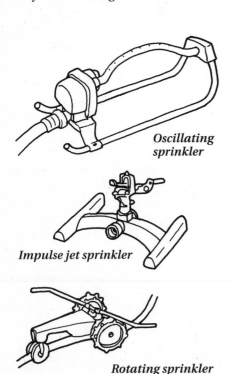

Oscillating sprinkler

Impulse jet sprinkler

Rotating sprinkler

A soaker hose will help you save significantly on your water bill. It can be adjusted to spray upward or downward.

Drip irrigation systems deliver water through emitters to individual plants. They are great for putting just the right amount of water where needed, but can be costly to install.

Soaker hoses and porous hoses deliver water along their length either through a series of holes, the soaker hose, or through the porous skin. Use some soaker hoses to water lawns as the holes are large enough to send water spraying upward. Turn them over so the water sprays downward to water vegetables or flowers. These hoses conserve water by putting it only where desired by the gardener. Place one along each garden row, or wind through flower beds and landscaping, to save time moving them around. Attach a garden hose when ready to water. Though a soaker hose is a bigger initial expense than a garden hose or cheap sprinkler, the savings on water can pay for the hoses in a couple of seasons. They also will last indefinitely.

Timers shut the water off at a pre-determined time. Cheap ones simply turn it off after a preset time period, while you can program expensive computer models with a complete watering regime. Both models

Electronic timer models

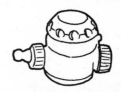

Inexpensive mechanical timer

prevent waste from overwatering, but the less expensive mechanical type is simpler to use and should be sufficient for almost anyone.

Water gauges measure how much water lands at a given spot. Save money by placing an empty jar or can in areas you want to measure.

Comforts and Conveniences

Some items just make gardening easier, and for that reason they may be worth the cost, but there are cheap substitutes you can use for quite a few of them.

Garden gloves protect your hands. Heavier material provides more protection. Cheap cloth gloves keep your hands clean. Heavy-duty leather gloves protect against thorns during pruning or brush-cutting, and guard against blisters after hours of hoeing or spading.

Knee pads or kneelers are valuable for anyone whose knees or back aches after weeding or performing other ground-work. Knee pads allow

Worthwhile Gardening Comforts

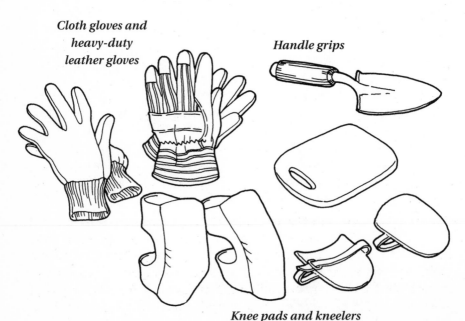

Cloth gloves and heavy-duty leather gloves

Handle grips

Knee pads and kneelers

more free movement than a kneeler that must be picked up and moved every few minutes as you move.

Handle grips are rubber tubes that fit over tool handles, such as hoes, rakes, and spades. They reduce wear on both handles and hands. For a cheap substitute wrap handles with foam pipe insulation, and attach the foam neatly with electrical tape.

Wheelbarrows haul soil, garden waste, and other loads from one place to another. The bed, constructed of metal, plastic, or wood, attaches to one or two wheels, depending on the design.

> **MONEY-SAVING TIP**
> For weeding substitute an old, plastic laundry basket, a five-gallon bucket, or an old canvas tote bag for a wheelbarrow.

For large or heavy loads, the two-wheeled version is the easiest to use. Metal won't crack like plastic, but it will rust.

Planting Aids

From starting seeds to maintaining full-grown plants, there is equipment for every step of the way. Almost anything you can buy for those jobs has a free or cheap substitute.

Seed-starting pots are available in plastic or peat. There is no reason to pay for either. (See Chapter 5 for alternatives.) Save pots and flats whenever you purchase plants and reuse them. If you purchase less plastic, then you will not have to pay to throw it away.

Soil thermometers can help you decide when to seed temperature-sensitive plants. However, with practice, and perhaps a little trial and error, you'll soon develop a "feel" for soil temperature that's just as dependable. Just touching the soil will tell you if it's warm enough to plant.

Dibbles make holes in soil for placing seeds. A stick, pencil, or finger performs the same.

Labels are useful for remembering what you planted. Make your own by cutting waxed milk cartons into strips and writing on the plain side with a permanent marker. Or push a stick through the seed packet and into the soil.

Plant ties and supports hold plants in place as they grow. Instead of using ties from the garden center, substitute cloth strips, plastic garbage bag ties, twine, or twist-ties, and your plants will never know the difference. Wire tomato cages are too small to support most mature tomato plants. They are great, though, as supports for many types of flowering plants. Use a pair of wire cutters to snip the cage just above the first horizontal wire for two small flower supports. For tomatoes and other vining crops, welded wire fencing, hopefully salvaged, makes a good support. Twine is great for many garden jobs, and it is often free from anyone who feeds baled hay to livestock. Metal fence posts are available in various lengths, are reasonably priced, will last forever, and will support the weight of any crop.

Plant protectors from waxed paper hot caps to entire greenhouses, can really extend the life of plants. (See pages 99–107.)

Proper Care for Longer Wear

The secret to protecting your investment in garden tools and equipment is taking good care of what you buy. Most important, clean all tools immediately after use and store them out of the weather.

Hoes, Spades, Shovels, Forks, Rakes, and Edgers

Two things this type of tool deserves are a place to call home and a bucket of oily sand. Mix a bottle of vegetable oil in with clean construction sand. After each use, hose off dirt and plunge the tool into the bucket with the sand and oil. The sand scours the metal, and the oil coats it preventing rust. Then hang up the tool in its proper spot. If the handles are wood, coat them with varnish, or rub with linseed or tung oil to preserve.

MONEY-SAVING TIP
Keep a bucket of oily sand nearby for keeping tools clean and rust-free.

Hoes, spades, shovels, and edgers perform better if the edge is sharp. File tools to a sharp edge at least once a year.

Pruners, Loppers, and Shears

The first rule is never misuse these cutting tools. They are meant to cut stems not wire. One wrong cut can ruin a good blade. Use soap and water to wash away sap or pitch; you may need a bit of turpentine or hand-cleaner for spots that are hard to remove. Scrub tool with steel wool to remove rust. Keep the moving parts lubricated with WD-40 or sewing machine oil. Check nuts and bolts periodically to make sure they are tight. Sharpen if cutting becomes difficult.

Power Equipment

Such a large investment deserves protection. The best advice is to follow the manufacturer's maintenance recommendations. Use only recommended fuel, change oil and filters on schedule, monitor spark plugs on gas models, and keep all blades sharp. Remove any debris from chippers, shredders, and lawn mowers before storing. Drain fuel before putting away for the winter.

Watering Equipment

The biggest threat to watering equipment is forgetful gardeners. Remember to disconnect, drain, and put away all hoses and sprinklers before a hard frost. If full of water, one hard freeze can split and ruin the best hoses. During the gardening season try to remember where you placed your hoses. It sounds easy enough, but how many gardeners ruin hoses by running over them with a lawn mower?

Repair or Replace

Proper maintenance goes a long way toward preventing premature tool damage. Eventually something is bound to break, get stuck, or become dull. Knowing how and when to repair rather than replace is important for the frugal gardener.

Stay Sharp

To sharpen equipment properly is a refined skill. You will need a vise, a file or whetstone, and a basic understanding of the function of the edge that you are sharpening.

Shovels, spades, and hoes get dull from digging through rocks. To sharpen, secure the head in a vise, don a pair of gloves, and grasp the file at both ends. A 10-inch mill bastard file works best. Run the file along the beveled rim of the shovel, applying force as you push forward and lifting up as you pull back. Only sharpen the beveled side.

The angle between the file and the head determines how strong or sharp the finished edge will be; a wider angle gives a stronger edge, and a narrow angle results in a sharper edge. Many gardeners prefer a strong edge on shovels

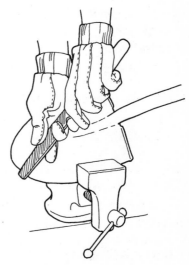

Sharpening your shovels will make them last longer and perform more effectively.

and a slicing one on hoes, but a 35- to 40-degree angle yields a sturdy, sharp blade.

Sharpen pruners or shears with a small, flat single-cut file or whetstone. Secure one handle in the vise and apply force only with the angle of the blades. Push the file from the hinged part of the blade to the tip. Never file along the flat side of by-pass or parrot-bill shears. The clean cut made by these pruners is the direct result of the beveled edge gliding closely along the flat; altering the flat side leaves a gap.

Lawn-mower blades should be sharpened once a year. To sharpen, remove blades if possible, or disconnect the spark plug wire for safety's sake, if sharpening on the mower. Using a bastard file, draw along the edge on either side, filing equally on each side to maintain balance.

Sharpening is not always the answer. Large nicks in any blade mean it's time for a replacement. On better pruners and loppers, you can adjust the anvils to make up for wear on the blades. Make sure the nut or bolt is tight.

Get a Handle on It

You can extend the life of any wooden handle the day you buy it. Use fine sandpaper to remove the finish. With your bare hands or a soft rag, generously rub the handle with boiled linseed oil. The warmth from your hands will help work in the oil, or leave a rag-oiled handle in the sun to warm the oil into the wood. Tung oil or vegetable oils such as olive or safflower oils also make good preservatives. The result is a smooth, water-resistant finish. Replenish with another rub whenever the wood begins to lose its satin feel.

Replace cracked shovel or fork handles. Digging puts a lot of stress on these tools, and having one give out at the wrong moment can be dangerous. Repair splits in hoe or rake handles by prying them open, filling with wood glue or epoxy, clamping till dry, and sanding smooth. It's usually quicker just to replace the handle. Don't ever try to get by with wrapping tape around a cracked handle. It is cheap, but it only hides a potentially worsening problem.

MONEY-SAVING TIP
Extend the life of your tools by keeping the handles in good condition, and replacing them when necessary.

Handles come in different styles, but the method of replacement is about the same. Begin by removing the old handle. There is usually a screw or rivet holding the handle in place. Take the screw or rivet out of the tool socket carefully, without altering the socket shape. You may have to bang the old handle out with a chunk of pipe.

Install the new handle by securing the tool head, spade or fork, in a vise and pushing the handle into the socket. Soak the handle in hot water or coat the socket with a little oil or soap to help the handle slide in easily, especially with curved sockets. Tap the handle as far as it will go. Prevent the new handle from ever flying free by drilling a hole and inserting a nut and bolt through the metal socket into the handle.

A Fix for Hoses

My hoses seem to get shorter every year. That's because rather than throw them away after accidentally smashing the couplings or cutting them in half, I repair them.

There are two types of repair kits available at garden centers. They differ in how to secure the coupling. One type uses prongs that clamp down around the end of the hose, and the other applies a band at the hose end.

First cut away the damaged coupling or shredded section of hose. Soak the hose end in hot water for a few minutes to soften. If using a band repair kit, slide the band over the hose, and insert the fitting. Tighten the band as close to the coupling as possible. To repair with a prong-type kit, insert the fitting, and clamp the prongs down as tightly as possible with a pair of pliers.

Dare to Repair?

Some items require repairs beyond the average gardener's ability, but still don't need to be replaced. Take mowers, tillers, shredders, and trimmers to a professional for repairs. If you attempt to fix the machine, it would void your warranty, take a lot of time, and possibly ruin your equipment.

You can mend other tools in a jiffy if you are willing to take the time and look at the problem. If you correct a small problem immediately, it won't become a big problem.

To Buy or Not to Buy

I had always wanted the biggest rototiller I could get. I still don't have it, and now you couldn't give me one. I did, however, buy myself a chipper/shredder for Mother's Day one year. What makes gardener's spring for these big-ticket items? What are the alternatives to buying?

For me the rototiller became a non-necessity when I changed gardening styles. By forming raised beds, I eliminated the need for a tiller, the soil stays soft, and is easy to turn with a spade in the spring. In fact, a tiller would make more work by tearing up the beds. But the shredder was different. Lots of barnyard critters, weeds, and pine cones add up to lots of waste that requires managing on a regular basis. The shredder makes quick work of turning mountains into molehills.

When considering adding tools to your gardening ensemble, take a hard look at how often you will use a new piece of equipment. If, like that heavy-duty rototiller, it will only see action a couple of times a year, think about renting one only when you need it. It is less convenient to pick it up, lug it home, and return it after use. But think about the perks. There are no maintenance costs, no storage, no parting with the purchase price, and you still save money. For example, a tiller, with a five-year warranty, sells for around $800. A similar machine rents for $40 an hour. You can rent that machine once a year for twenty years, or twice a year for ten years, before you spend the amount it would cost to buy it. Other "occasional-use" equipment you might consider renting include the chipper/shredder, hedge trimmers, and leaf blower.

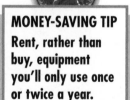

MONEY-SAVING TIP
Rent, rather than buy, equipment you'll only use once or twice a year.

Neighborly cooperation can go a long way to saving money as well. Get a nearby gardening friend or two to share your rental. Most rental companies charge just as much for the half-hour it takes to drive the machine home as they do for the time it is in use. By splitting the expense with others, you cut down on wasted rental time.

New or Used

If you have a Sunday newspaper handy, check the classified ads for used gardening equipment. From chippers to string trimmers, used equipment is a respectable market. Also look at yard sales and estate sales for used equipment.

When should you consider buying used equipment? The answer is if you are in the market for an item, and you find that the same investment will buy a better quality used machine than a new one. This is not all that unusual. Ask why the equipment is for sale. Two common reasons are the owner has either given up on gardening, or has purchased a more advanced model of machinery. Neither means there is anything necessarily wrong with the machine for sale.

New vs. Used Equipment

When purchasing either new or used equipment, consider the following trade-offs to get the most for your money.

NEW	USED
Advantages	**Advantage**
Warranty.	Cheaper.
Broad choice of machines and options.	**Disadvantages**
No wear on working parts.	No warranty.
Clean and shiny. Looks great.	May be worn out.
Service available when needed.	May need repairs.
	Will have to find someone to service it.
Disadvantages	
Expensive.	

What to Ask About Used Equipment

The gamble of buying used equipment is you may just be getting someone else's headache. Without being too intrusive, you may want to approach this by asking if the seller still plans to garden. If so, then either the equipment no longer suits his purposes, or the gardener's sick of it!

Get as much information as possible from the seller about a piece of equipment you're considering buying. Following are some good questions to ask.

1. What is the make, model, and year of the machine? A used machine may have a warranty in effect.
2. What was the maintenance schedule?
3. Has the machine been adjusted or repaired?
4. Where can you take the machine for service when needed?
5. Why is the equipment for sale? (You may even get an honest answer.)

After you have gleaned as much information as possible from the seller, call a local dealer. Grill the dealer for information, especially on potential problems of that particular machine. Ask about specific things to look for in a used model.

What to Look For

Ask yourself some general questions when looking at a used machine. Does it *appear* to have been well-maintained? Is it reasonably clean? Ask the seller to check the oil, and other applicable fluids or lubrication points. This will show you if the machine is currently in good condition. Also if a seller is not familiar enough with the machine to do this for you, he probably didn't perform routine maintenance. Ask for a "test drive." Evaluate how easily it starts, how comfortable it is for you to use, and how efficient the machine is for the type of job you have at home. Ask where you can take the machine for servicing, if necessary. This applies for new or used equipment, since not all places that sell garden equipment service what they sell. For specific tools, new or used, look for the following characteristics.

Chipper/shredders. Consider maneuverability, balance, the clutch system, and ease of feeding material into it. You don't want to lift heavy materials or shovel loads over your head to use the machine. A grate to regulate the size of material as it comes out will eliminate running material through twice.

Rototillers. Rear-tine machines are generally the easiest for most people to operate. After test driving, does the machine leave a well-prepared, fluffy seed-bed?

Lawn mowers. Variable speed drive offers a choice of working conditions, which is valuable because grass and mowing conditions vary. Opt for a mulching type of lawn mower if possible. Not only are they the most efficient, but they also are the most environmentally responsible. If looking at self-propelled mowers, try to find one with at least a five-horsepower motor. For the difference in price, it will last a lot longer than a smaller engine. For machines with baggers, test the bag. Look for ease of handling, removing, and emptying when full. If your yard is fairly even and free of debris, consider a push-reel mower.

String Trimmers. Try one long enough to determine if it is comfortable for you to use. Is it well balanced or too heavy? Correctly match the machine to your job at home. For grass edging, a small, curve-shaft trimmer should suffice. A mid-size trimmer will be more effective for weeds, but clearing the back forty acres may require a heavy-duty, two-handled model.

Hedge Trimmers. Make sure the tool can be sharpened; many cannot. Consider how much it weighs. Is it too heavy for you to operate comfortably for extended periods of time?

Leaf Blowers. Air speed and the volume of air the machine moves are equally important. Check the consistency of the sweep. Does it move material equally well at the edges and the center? If the machine has a vacuum attachment make sure material is not forced back through the fan blades.

3

PRICELESS PLANTS

Take a look at your plant budget. What plant budget, you ask. Most gardeners always seem to scrape up just enough cash or credit to buy one more interesting plant, or one more packet of seed. Setting a limit on spending somehow seems ungardener-like. Wouldn't it be nice if you could cut the cost but still have all the plants you want?

Free Seeds

Compared to the overall cost of gardening, seed is really a bargain. But why pay for them when they are all around you for free? If you have plants, you have seeds. You should know, however, that seeds from hybrid plants don't produce plants just like their parents. Hybrids are the result of cross-fertilization between two or more species. Open-pollinated plants, on the other hand, are fertilized naturally — "in the open" — and are likely to produce offspring similar to the parent plant. If you plan to collect seed for future seasons' plantings, you will have better results if you choose seeds or plants that are labelled "open-pollinated" or "OP" in a catalog or nursery.

The seed-saving process is simple and basically the same for all seed-bearing plants.

How to Save Your Own Seeds

Step 1: Let one or more plants of a chosen variety go to seed. First the plant must flower, then fruit, such as a tomato, pea-pod, rose-hip, apple, or seed head will form. Leave on the plant until it is past ripe or about to fall off.

Step 2: Pick fruit or seed head. Remove seeds.

Step 3: Dry seeds thoroughly before packaging in envelopes or airtight containers.

Step 4: Label and store seeds in a cool, dry place.

Step 5: When ready to use, test seeds for germination.

Step 6: Sow.

Annuals are the easiest plants from which to collect seed. Start with them if you are new to the practice. Many perennials are also easy to propagate from seed. Since biennials don't flower or set seed until their second year, they may require protection over the winter to stay alive long enough to yield seed.

Going to Seed

The first step in seed-saving is to let your plants produce the seed. Choose the very best example of each type of plant as the parent for the next generation. Look for good color, fine flavor, superior size, texture, or yield, and disease or insect resistance. In short, choose plants with unique qualities that set them apart from the rest. Never collect seed from diseased plants, because some diseases are seed-borne. Growing conditions during seed development affect the quality of seeds, so take good care of the expectant plants.

To set seed, the plant must be pollinated. Some plants, such as beans, lettuce, peas, and tomatoes are self-pollinating, which means the flowers on the plant produce and accept their own pollen. Others require pollen from a second plant, delivered either by the breeze or the bees. This can complicate seed-saving when related plants cross-pollinate, thereby affecting the seed crop.

In the garden, usually only plants of the same species can cross-pollinate. If you grow several varieties of a species, cover selected plants, or individual flowers, to prevent cross-pollination. For wind-pollinated crops, such as beets, chard, corn, and spinach, use muslin or spun-bonded

When you are planning to save seeds, you may want to prevent cross-polination of crops such as broccoli by covering them with cheese cloth. This keeps the insects away, but requires that you then polinate plants by hand.

polypropylene to keep away the tiny grains of pollen. For insect-pollinated crops, such as broccoli, carrots, or squash, cheesecloth will keep the bugs away from the flowers.

Once you cover plants that are normally pollinated by insects, you become responsible for their pollination. They can be hand-pollinated by gently stroking flowers with a fine artist's paintbrush.

The process becomes simpler if you grow only one variety of each plant, or if you don't mind the effects of crossing two cultivars.

Often a cross between two types, say of tomatoes or carrots, doesn't result in any tremendous surprises. But let two cultivars of the species *Cucurbita pepo* — pumpkins, zucchini, scallop, crooknecks, acorn squash, spaghetti squash, and some gourds — mingle, and you could find some real oddballs in next year's pumpkin patch.

PLANTS SUITABLE FOR SEED-SAVING

ANNUALS	PERENNIALS	BIENNIALS
Beans	Artichokes	Beets
Broccoli	Asparagus	Brussels sprouts
Cucumbers	Chives	Cabbage
Dill	Flowers	Carrots
Eggplant	Herbs (many)	Cauliflower
Flowers	Rhubarb	Celery
Lettuce	Roses	Kale
Melons	Shrubs	Parsley
Okra	Trees	Rutabagas
Onions		Turnips
Peas		
Peppers		
Pumpkins		
Radishes		
Spinach		
Squash		
Tomatoes		

Collecting Seeds

Once you have seeds, the next step is to gather and prepare them for storage. For most plants, it is critical to wait until the seeds are ripe before you harvest them. Failure to do so results in seeds with a low germination rate and poor vigor. Some exceptions are snap beans, lettuce, radishes, spinach, and tomatoes, which germinate fairly well when a little underripe. Although the seeds must be ripe, it also is important to make sure they are not yet rotten or expelled by the plant when harvesting. A dry, sunny day is perfect for gathering seeds or seed fruit.

The method of harvest depends on the type of plant. Many annual flowers, lettuce, and onions release their seeds as soon as they mature. Tie a small paper bag over the developing seed head to catch them as they fall. Wait until fleshy fruits, such as melons, tomatoes, rose hips, shrub berries, or tree fruit, are a little overripe to pick. Scrape the seeds from the flesh of the fruit, soak to remove any residue, and allow to dry completely. Some plants produce capsules or seed pods; snap them off, break open, and shake the seeds out over white paper.

The moisture content of stored seeds is critical to their viability. (Viability determines whether or not it will sprout.) Seeds must be kept as dry as possible. Spread clean seeds out on newspapers in a dry place for at least one week. Hang an incandescent lightbulb overhead to raise the temperature slightly and dry the surrounding air. Temperatures much over 100°F as well as any other factors causing the seeds to dry too quickly will damage them. Some seeds will dry just fine on the plant; poppy seeds and peas are good examples. An alternate method is to wrap the seeds in paper, and place in a jar with an equal weight of silica gel. Small seeds will dry in about ten days, while larger ones can take up to sixteen days. Test for dryness by bending the seeds. Those that snap back are not ready for storage, but those that break are ready.

HOW TO COLLECT VEGETABLE SEEDS

Asparagus.   Only female plants produce the berries which contain seeds. Harvest when berries turn red.

Beans & Peas.   Leave the pods on the plant until dry.

Broccoli.   Let buds flower and develop until pods form. Collect after the pods have dried on the plant.

Cabbage.   This biennial sends up seed stalk which develops pods. Pick after pods have turned yellow.

Carrot . Seeds on this biennial ripen about 60 days after flowering. Carrots cross with the weed Queen Anne's Lace, so don't allow it nearby.

Cauliflower. Pick after pods turn brown.

Corn. Different varieties cross-pollinate. Keep them separated by at least 100 feet or cover ears with a paper bag before the silks emerge. Hand-pollinate by covering tassels with a paper bag to collect pollen, and then by sprinkling pollen over silks. Allow the ears to ripen on the plant. Husk corn, and hang it until kernels are dry.

Cucumbers. Different cultivars cross-pollinate, so isolate them. Pick after cucumbers turn yellow. Scrape out seed pulp and wash seeds.

Dill. Let seeds dry on plant.

Eggplant. Pick when fruit turns dull and wrinkly. Separate seeds from flesh.

Lettuce. Wait for the last plants to bolt, then let flower. Harvest when fluffy, white seeds form.

Melons. Harvest fruit when ripe, scrape out seeds, rinse, and dry.

Okra. Allow pods to ripen on plant.

Onion. Harvest flowering tops as soon as black seeds are visible. Dry for a few weeks, then gently rub off the seeds.

Peppers. Wait until the fruit has reached the appropriate color for its variety; most turn red. Cut off the top of the pepper and shake or scoop out seeds.

Potatoes. Seeds do develop, but planting from seed potatoes is easiest. Dig up future seed potatoes and let dry in the sun to improve storage. Never do this with eating spuds, because they turn green and bitter.

Pumpkins & Squash. Allow fruit to ripen fully and scrape out seeds.

Radishes. Let flower and harvest when seed pods are dry.

Spinach. Let seeds ripen on plants.

Sunflowers. Allow them to dry on the stalk. You may need to cover sunflowers to protect from birds.

Tomatoes. Pick overripe fruit; squeeze pulp and seeds into a jar. Allow to ferment at room temperature for three or four days. Stir daily and pour off any liquid and floating seeds. Keep only the seeds that sink; rinse and dry them.

Turnips. Dig up this biennial, and overwinter 1-year-old plants in a root cellar. Replant in spring for seed production. Harvest seed pods when dry.

Storing Seeds

You can find good, cheap containers for storing seeds around your house, including old prescription bottles, glass jars with screw-on lids, and plastic film cannisters. These containers all protect from outside moisture and pests. If you have some very small packets of seeds, label and store them within a larger container.

Seeds must be kept dry and cool, otherwise they rot or sprout. Humidity of less than 60 percent, and temperatures between 32°F and 41°F are ideal. Add a packet of desiccant powder (such as silica gel) or powdered milk, to combat high humidity. The gel absorbs best. Under good conditions, many types of seed will remain viable for years.

══ VEGETABLE SEEDS: STORAGE LIFE AND VIABILITY ══

Seed	Years	Seed	Years
Asparagus	3	Muskmelons	5
Beans	3	Okra	2
Beets	4	Onions, Parsley	1
Broccoli, Brussels		Parsnips	1
sprouts, Cabbage	5	Peas	3
Carrots	3	Peppers	2
Cauliflower, Celery	5	Pumpkins	4
Corn	2	Radishes	5
Cucumbers	5	Spinach	5
Eggplant	5	Squash, Tomatoes	4
Lettuce	3		

The longer you store seeds, the less viable and vigorous they will be. The following table lists some common seeds and their storage life expectancies. Commercially packed seed may store longer than home-grown.

Testing Stored Seeds

Faster germination results in more vigorous plants. For this to occur a high percentage of the seeds should sprout within the normal time for its type. To determine how well your seeds have survived storage, perform a germination test.

Moisten a paper towel or coffee filter, place ten or twenty seeds on it, and seal in a zip-seal plastic bag. Open daily to check for germination. After the appropriate amount of time has passed for that type of seed, count the number of sprouts to figure the percentage.

Five out of ten seeds and ten out of twenty seeds gives a 50 percent rate. More seeds in the test will yield more accurate results. Seeds that show a better than 70 percent germination rate are average, over 80 percent are good, and better than 90 percent are great to plant.

DAYS TO GERMINATION FOR STORED SEEDS

Seed	Days at Room Temperature	Seed	Days at Room Temperature
Ageratum	5	Marigold	5
Asparagus	7 to 21	Nasturtium	8
Beans	6 to 14	Pansy	10
Beets	6 to 14	Parsley	14 to 28
Broccoli	3 to 10	Peppers	10 to 20
Cabbage	4 to 10	Primrose	25
Calendula	10	Pumpkins	6 to 10
Carrot	10 to 17	Radish	3 to 10
Cauliflower	4 to 10	Salvia	15
Chard	7 to 10	Snapdragon	10
Cosmos	5	Spinach	6 to 14
Cucumber	6 to 10	Summer squash	3 to 12
Eggplant	7 to 14	Tomato	6 to 14
Impatiens	15	Winter squash	6 to 10
Lettuce	4 to 10	Zinnia	5 to 7
Lobelia	20		

Don't bother planting poorly germinating seeds. They won't produce superior plants, a necessity for getting the most from your gardening dollar. Always start with the best seed possible, even if you have to go out and buy it.

Sowing Saved Seeds

The final step toward renewing your plant population is to sow the seeds. Chapter 6 describes how to start seeds and when to transplant. There is one other consideration, however, with home-cured seeds. Some types need a little help to sprout.

Most vegetable seeds don't need special attention to germinate. Soaking large vegetable seeds for one to two hours helps accelerate the process, but it is not absolutely necessary. Most flowers also don't require special treatment. A few perennial and shrub seeds, however, have unusual requirements.

Certain seeds, such as yarrow, or some varieties of aster or dianthus, remain dormant for a long time and will germinate best after their second year in storage. Others, such as some forms of primula or rhododendron, only germinate well when sowed fresh. Soaking seeds of camellia, cystitus, and other shrubs greatly enhances their germination rates.

Some seeds, such as those of lupine or peonies, are so tough they should be scarified. This means gently nicking or sanding the seed coat to give the embryo an escape route.

Let's Hear It for Self-Sowers

Some plants just won't give you the satisfaction of saving and using your own seed. They are do-it-yourselfers or self-sowers. If you don't pluck every last spent blossom from plants such as calendula, French marigolds, forget-me-nots, or sweet alyssum, they will seed themselves back. Personally, I like this approach. You not only save money, but also time and effort.

Often second-generation seeds won't grow up to look just like their parents, which is fine as long as they produce interesting or attractive plants. When weeding in the spring look for familiar seedlings, lest you accidently cull volunteer flowers (self-sown plants that pop up unexpectedly).

Self-Sowing Plants: What Will They Look Like?

Allowing plants to self-sow can save you money, time, and effort. But you have to be prepared for some surprises. Here's a brief guide to well-known self-sowers.

Will Grow True to Type:
Blue Cornflower, Calendula, Dill, French Marigold, Godetia, Love-in-a-Mist, Nasturtiums, Sweet Alyssum, Yellow Corydalis, Violets, Pansies.

Type Will Change With New Generation:
Forget-me-not, Foxglove, Snapdragon.

Plant Parenthood

For many types of plants, there are faster, inexpensive ways to cultivate new specimens than waiting for seeds to form and grow. Vegetative propagation means starting a new plant from an appropriate piece of an old one. Several methods exist, including taking cuttings, layering, dividing, and separating bulbs.

Cuttings

I love to take cuttings. Half the fun is that I get a new, free plant. The other half is that I almost always make a new friend, or strengthen the bond with an old one.

Taking cuttings is easy. It's a step-by-step procedure with varying rates of success, depending on the plant and your proficiency. Getting cuttings is another story. If you already have plants of which you want more, of course, it's simple. But if the plant of your dreams is in a stranger's yard or a park, the acquisition becomes not only a challenge, but also an opportunity.

There will always be exceptions, but few gardeners object to a friendly compliment about their plantings. And what greater compliment than to so admire something another gardener has grown, that you politely ask for a cutting? It can be a doubly rewarding experience;

How to Take Stem Cuttings

Step 1: With a sharp knife, slice the stem of the parent plant approximately 1 inch beneath a node.

Step 2: If you must transport the cutting, gently wrap it in a moistened, absorbent paper towel.

Step 3: Trim end of stem to just below a node. Often you can take several cuttings from each collected stem. Snip off any flowers and all but two or three leaves.

Taking the cutting.

Step 4: Dip in rooting hormone, if desired. These products prompt root cells to divide. Place cuttings in moist rooting medium. Some plants, such as pelargonium and coleus, will root in a glass of water.

Step 5: Cover cuttings with plastic.

Step 6: Pot or transplant cuttings when new growth shows.

Transplanted cutting.

you get plants and make friends. If you appear presentable, courteous, and knowledgeable, you will assuage any fears that you might damage their precious plants. Offer to propagate a cutting for the gardener, as well as yourself. This one almost always works!

Take cuttings from the stem, leaves, or roots of various plant species. Stem cuttings are referred to as softwood, greenwood, or hardwood. Softwood cuttings are those taken in the spring before new growth begins to harden. They are the easiest to root.

Greenwood cuttings are taken in the summer before the stems have fully matured. They root a little slower, but on average are more likely to survive. Hardwood cuttings are taken from mature stems at the end of the growing season. They are usually the slowest to root. Leaf cuttings, reserved for fleshy-leaved plants, can be taken anytime during the growing season. Root cuttings are taken from dormant shrubs or trees. Often one method works better than the others for a specific plant; even varieties within a species respond differently.

Cutting a piece from a plant and having a whole new plant form may seem like magic to non-gardeners, comparable to cutting off your finger and growing a twin.

PLANTS SUITABLE FOR SOFTWOOD STEM CUTTINGS

FRUIT	CLIMBERS	SHRUBS	TREES
Blueberries	Black-eyed	Butterfly bush	American
Gauvas	Susan vine	Flowering	sweet gum
Pomegranates	Clematis,	maple	Birch
	some	Forsythia	Catalpa
PERENNIALS*	Climbing	Fuschia	Colesium
	hydrangea	Heath	maple
Aubrieta	Glorybower	Hydrangea	Flowering
Dianthus	Hedera ivy	Lantana	plum and
Phlox	Hedera	Philadelphis	cherry
Primula	(English) ivy	Potentilla	Ginkgo bilboa
Verbena	Honeysuckle	Roses	Goldenrain
Viola	Hoya black-	Viburnum	tree
	eyed susan		Smoke tree
	vine		
	Ivy geranium		
	Morning glory		
	Trumpet vines		
	(various		
	species)		*(lists continue on next page)*

*Take stem cuttings whenever shoots are available.

PLANTS SUITABLE FOR GREENWOOD STEM CUTTINGS

CLIMBERS	PERENNIALS	SHRUBS	TREES
Clematis, some species	Clematis	Barberry	Arborvitae
Euonymus	Daphne	Bottlebrush	Cedar
Grapes, some species	Pelargonium	Camellia	Cypress
Honeysuckle	Helianthemum	Cotoneaster	False cypress
Trumpet vine	Veronica	Daphne	Hemlock
		Holly	Holly
		Oregon grape	Juniper
		Rhododen-dron	Magnolia
		Roses	Privet
		Rose of Sharon	
		Russian olive	
		Viburnum	
		Weigela	

PLANTS SUITABLE FOR HARDWOOD STEM CUTTINGS

CLIMBERS	FRUIT	SHRUBS	TREES
Bougainvillea	Blueberries	Boxwood	Dawn redwood
Honeysuckle, some	Currants	Butterfly bush	Ficus
Kolomikta kiwi	Figs	Cotoneaster	Mulberry
Virginia creeper	Gooseberries	Dogwood	Poplar
	Grapes	Elderberry	Sycamore
	Raspberries	Forsythia	Willow
		Japanese aucuba	
		Mock orange	
		Privet	
		Rosa rugosa	
		Spirea	
		Viburnum	
		Weigela	

PLANTS SUITABLE FOR LEAF CUTTINGS

African violet	Hen and chicks
Begonia	Peperomia
Cape primrose	Sedum
Gloxinia	

How to Take Leaf Cuttings

Step 1: Cut a healthy leaf from the parent plant.

Step 2: If you must transport it, wrap leaf in moist towel.

Step 3: Place it in moist rooting medium. There are different ways to do this. The leaf may be set upright so the blade is in contact with the rooting medium. You also can cut several nicks along the length of the veins, and press the leaf flat, vein-side down in the rooting medium. Or cut the leaf lengthwise and insert into rooting medium with the cut-side down to expose the veins.

Step 4: Cover with clear plastic.

Step 5: Water it and keep away from direct sunlight.

Step 6: Pot new plants after a few leaves appear.

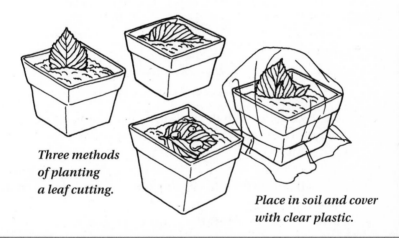

Three methods of planting a leaf cutting.

Place in soil and cover with clear plastic.

If you master the art of taking stem cuttings, you may find yourself suddenly surrounded by new plants. Some plants root more easily than others. If a cutting doesn't root well in the spring, try again later in the season. Since plants mature at different rates, in different climes, and even in different years, there always will be some variability. Keep records to refine the practice for your area.

This method of creating free plants is well-suited to houseplants. Roots form along the veins and usually several new plantlets emerge from each leaf cutting.

Layering

Layering stems to produce new plants is almost too easy. By either covering a section of stem with soil or simulating that effect, the stem sprouts roots. Once rooted, the stem can be separated from the parent plant and transplanted.

Simple layering works best during the dormant season. Cut a small nick into the bottom side of a stem and anchor it into prepared soil, either on the ground or in a pot. It helps to stake the tip of the stem.

═══ PLANTS SUITABLE FOR TAKING ROOT CUTTINGS ═══

PERENNIALS

Anchusa azurea
Bellflowers
Blanket flower
Bluebells
Creeping phlox
Cupid's dart

Some geraniums
Globeflower
Japanese
  anemone
Oriental poppy

SHRUBS

Bayberry
Glorybower
Pacific wax myrtle
Sumac

How to Take Root Cuttings

Step 1: Gently dig through the soil to expose young, growing roots, approximately pencil-size. Herbaceous perennials may be thinner.

Step 2: With a sharp knife cut the root straight across, and place an angled cut further down the root. This way you can tell which end is up.

Step 3: If you must transport the cutting, wrap it in a moist paper towel.

Step 4: Remove any fibrous roots. You can divide long cuttings and shorten thinner ones to between 3 and 5 inches. Make a fresh, slanted cut in each piece to designate top and bottom.

Step 5: Dip cutting into rooting hormone.

Step 6: Insert cutting into moist rooting medium with the slanted end down and the straight-cut-end level with the surface. For thin roots, lay them sideways, and cover lightly with soil. You can root some species, such as lilac and sumac, directly into the garden site.

Step 7: Pot or transplant roots after a few leaves develop.

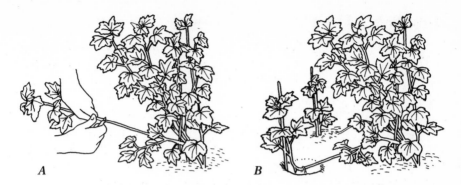

Layering a plant's stem by (A) nicking it and (B) covering it with soil will produce new plants.

Leave it alone, except to water, until the end of the next growing season. If the roots are strong, then cut the new plant from the parent and transplant.

A variation, called serpentine layering, involves anchoring a long stem to the soil in several spots. It's a great way to make several copies of plants, such as clematis or climbing roses, that send out long, flexible stems.

Some plants, raspberry and blackberry varieties in particular, reproduce readily by tip-layering. It works like simple layering, except you bury the tip of the vine.

Another technique is air layering, whereby you trick the stem into believing it has been anchored in the soil. Remove any leaves that are in the way. Make a sleeve from plastic wrap and fit it over or around the stem; wrap the bottom with tape. Make a slanted cut upwards into the stem with a sharp knife, and quickly pack around the stem with moist sphagnum moss using the back of the knife. Pull the sleeve up, pack fully with more damp moss, and seal the top of the plastic sleeve firmly with tape. Eventually roots will show through the plastic. At this point, cut the stem off just below the new root ball and pot up the new plant.

Divide and Multiply

Dividing is a quick way to multiply your collection of perennials, succulents, and some suckering shrubs. Dividing yields two or more plants from one, and it is healthier for the original plant than being left to overcrowd itself.

The best time to divide most plants is from late fall to early spring. Avoid especially cold or wet periods as these make it tough for the divided plants to reestablish. Plants with fleshy roots, such as irises,

PLANTS SUITABLE FOR LAYERING

SIMPLE	SERPENTINE	TIP	AIR
Akebia	Bittersweet	Trailing	Citrus
Campsis	Blueberry	blackberries	Ficus
Forsythia	climber	Raspberries	Magnolia
Honeysuckle	Campsis		Mountain
Potentilla	Clematis		laurel
Rhododen-			
dron			
Roses			
Wisteria			

Air Layering

Step 1: Make a slanted cut upwards into the stem.

Step 2: Pack the cut stem with sphagnum moss.

Step 3: Pull up the plastic sleeve and seal the top and bottom with tape.

Step 4: When roots show through the plastic. Cut the bottom stem off.

peonies, and poppies, have a better chance of rooting if divided in late summer.

Begin by gently digging around the base of the plant to expose the perimeters of it. Then carefully lift the plant with a garden fork. Shake or brush off as much soil as possible so you can see what you are doing. Often with older plants, there will be a dead spot of brown stems in the center of the plant. Cut this out and divide the remaining growth. The simplest way to divide most plants is to grasp large sections by hand and gently, but firmly, pull them apart. Plants that can't be pulled apart can be cut through with a sharp spade. Make sure you leave a few buds on each division.

You can dust any cuts with a fungicide to curb infection. Cut back the tops and place the new plants in the ground at the same height they were growing before, and water.

Bulbs, Corms, and Tubers

These are underground plant parts used to store energy for the coming year. Plants that grow from bulbs include common favorites, such as crocus, daffodil, narcissus, and tulips, as well as a range of others. They routinely develop offsets, smaller versions of themselves that you can separate from the parent.

Reap the bounty of tiny bulbs by lifting a clump with a fork and carefully pulling the bulblets free. Pot them and let grow for a year or two before planting outside. Some of the more common bulbs reproduce as follows:

→ **Lilies** form little bulbs along the length of the stem, which you can pluck and plant.
→ **Gladiolus** grow from corms, similar to underground bulbs, and you can separate them the same way.
→ **Dahlias** grow from large, fleshy tubers. In most parts of the country, you must dig them up every fall and bring them in from the cold. In the spring, as buds form, cut the tuber into sections. Make sure you include a couple of buds on each section.

Bulb offsets can be separated and planted individually.

Slightly Used Plants

Another way to save on plant costs is to "reuse" grown plants from your own garden, or those unwanted by others.

One of the best reasons to belong to a garden club, apart from the friendship, is that members give each other or sell cheaply perfectly good plants. Plant swaps or sales are standard among clubs and a great way to increase your plant collection. If you're not a member of a formal club, create the same opportunities simply by talking with others about your garden and theirs. Once people know you are a plant nut, they offer you all kinds of plant items.

Moving Established Plants

Plants move around some people's yards more than the people. A shrub just doesn't prosper in a particular corner. A rose bush might clash with a climbing vine. It's actually a lot like moving furniture around until you create just the perfect setting in your outdoor room. Furniture doesn't suffer transplant shock, however. The first rule of thumb for digging up and relocating any plant is to wait until the plant is dormant. This causes the least possible amount of stress on the plant. Fall is usually the best time. For most perennials, dig down around the perimeter of the plant to create a rootball large enough to accommodate the plant. For shrubs and trees, a burlap wrap will help hold the rootball in place. Dig a trench around the perimeter of the plant branches, the dripline, and use a fork or spade to pull as much soil away from roots as possible to create a ball of soil. Tip the rootball up with the edge of a shovel, and shuffle the burlap underneath. Repeat around the plant, shifting the burlap until it encircles the roots. For heavy shrubs or trees, you may need to slide a board or two underneath the rootball to create enough leverage to move the plant. Lift the plant carefully and transport.

MONEY-SAVING TIP
To find great deals on grown plants, join your local garden club and participate in their plant swaps and sales.

You can dig up plants routinely sold bare root — such as roses, grapes, raspberries, blueberries, and many shrubs — and treat them the same way as a bare-root transplant (See Chapter 5, pages 82–86). A younger plant has better chances of survival.

Where to Find Homeless Plants

Digging up someone else's landscape is obviously a bad idea, but there are a number of valuable resources for finding unwanted plants. Landscape companies frequently redesign existing plantings, both residential and commercial. Construction firms remove existing plants everyday when expanding structures, usually with a bulldozer. If you make contact with these people and offer to remove unwanted plants for free, you may find yourself with more plants than you can handle.

No matter what the source of a secondhand plant, transplant only healthy-looking specimens. A free diseased plant can become quite costly.

Seedy Deals

Mail-order catalogs and display racks everywhere from garden centers to grocery and hardware stores sell seeds. Which sources offer the best bargains?

Finding Seed Bargains

Mail-order seed companies are big business. Pick up a catalog and wander through those glossy pages of perfect plants; you can't help but be tempted to order many. Rule number one is to take the pictures with a grain of salt. Your plants probably won't look just like the picture-perfect ones.

Compare several catalogs, and you will quickly find that most are selling the same seeds, packaged a little differently in a range of prices. Look for the best-priced varieties with the color, flavor, texture, growth habit, or other traits you desire. Hint: It's not always the biggest company that offers the smallest price. Furthermore small seed companies often focus on local conditions and offer varieties that will thrive in your immediate area. Check them first if there are any near you.

Gardening magazines often have a seed-savers exchange section. Someone has saved variety X and would like to trade for Y. These are a great way to get seeds — often rare or heirloom varieties that are hard to find elsewhere. There are seed-saving clubs, such as the Seed Savers Exchange, the members of which trade thousands of seed varieties. (See page 156 for address.) Finally, plant associations abound for nearly every kind of plant — from alpines to water lilies. National groups usually send out a newsletter in which members often list plants they have to offer. If you have a real

MONEY-SAVING TIP
To save money on seeds and increase your selection, join a seed-savers exchange club.

passion for a particular kind of plant, get involved with the local chapter of the appropriate association. (Of course, the *really cheap* way is to become friends with someone who is already a member and borrow a copy of the newsletter!)

Two More Tricks to Cheap Seeds

Once upon a time I ran a bedding plant business. I think I made about $200 that year. But from that experience I learned something so obvious it's embarrassing. Wholesale is cheaper than retail. And nowhere is that more obvious than in the seed business.

Chapter 10 discusses ways to sell your produce and plants, but before you can sell them, you must buy seed. Owning a small greenhouse business has its advantages, not the least of which is you get to write things off on your taxes and maybe even realize a profit. You also get to buy from wholesale distributors. The price is always much less than retail. The catch is you must buy in quantity. This is not really a problem since most seed keeps for years, or you could resell some, perhaps at a reasonable mark-up, to gardening pals.

If you are not interested in going into business, then watch those seed-rack displays. Seed companies only sell seed packaged for the current year. At the end of each season, you can get mega-bargains on this year's product. Often seeds that sold for $1 a packet, sell at ten packets for $1 when the stores are clearing inventory. Garden centers offer the least drastic discounts, while grocery stores, hardware stores, and other stores not normally in the garden supply business just want to get rid of them. A word of caution, however, is remember that the perfect environment for storing seed is a cool, dry place. Don't buy from seed racks exposed to rain or excess summer heat. The seed may be ruined.

MONEY-SAVING TIP
Buy discounted seeds at the end of the season to save for the following year.

Nursery Shopping Strategy

The very best way to get top-quality plants from your local garden center or nursery is to get the best service. The people who work there are your most valuable resource. They know the quality of their product, their wholesalers, when the plants arrived, how they were cared for, and any problems that may exist. Do yourself a favor; get to know these folks.

Know When to Shop

Plants arrive at the garden center from the supplier in the best possible condition, given the rigors of shipment. They sometimes go downhill from there. When scouting for plants, call and ask when the store expects to receive their shipment from their best supplier, and show up when the plants arrive. Not only will you get the healthiest possible plants, but you will also get first pick.

You won't get a bargain if you wait for plants to go on sale. If a plant has been sitting on a rack for months, especially if it doesn't receive proper care, then it probably won't amount to much. The best bets among such plants are perennials, but only if the price is *really low.* If you feel you can bring a plant around, then by all means take a cheap gamble. Otherwise, spend wisely, and buy early.

Signs of a Good Investment

Blossoms are the one feature that attract buyers most readily. Yet seedlings that have been forced into bloom in order to make them more tempting to buyers can actually result in less productive plants in the long run. The stress of life with few roots and a big head slows plant vigor.

Look for compact, vigorous plants that appear healthy. Pass by plants with dead or yellowing leaves or those that have grown leggy. Be wary of unstable stems or plants that look poorly rooted. Well-rooted plants will recover from transplant shock much more quickly than those with poorly developed roots. If you can find plants that are not yet in bloom, consider them first.

MONEY-SAVING TIP
Find out when a nursery is expecting a new shipment so you can shop for the healthiest plants.

When buying perennials always look at the roots, because that is the future of the plant. A healthy root system ensures the plant will live to bloom for years to come.

No matter what type of plant you are buying, look it over thoroughly for any signs of pests or diseases. Never buy sick or infested plants at any price.

4

WINNING VARIETIES

No matter what you pay for plants, unless they suit your particular needs, they are not a good investment. Even free plants require time and expense you cannot afford to waste on disappointing specimens. Some plants require less coddling than others do, and offer more in return.

Go Native

The plants best suited to your area are those nature put there. Check with your County Extension Service for ideas and sources. The trick to incorporating native plants is to get rid of any images of perfectly mowed grass surrounded by a neatly trimmed hedge. Wander out into the country and look at how nature arranges plants. A word of caution is necessary here. Not only is it bad manners to go out and lift plants from the wild, in many cases it is downright illegal. Check with your local Audubon Society Chapter or native plant society to determine whether a plant is endangered. Removing endangered plants from the wild is prohibited, and even collecting seeds from such plants may be restricted. In the case of others, you must have permission from a private property owner before digging up desirable natives. You can, however, make note of the plants you want, and gather seeds in the fall.

Not All Natives Are Locals

Going native doesn't necessarily mean including *only* local plants in the landscape. Your hometown surely is unique, but there are other regions throughout the world with similar climates — latitude, altitude, and distance from large bodies of water. Plants from similar zones often grow equally as well in one as in another. For instance, Rugosa roses, native to the Far East, thrive in seaboard towns everywhere. Alpine plants from Switzerland flourish in rock gardens in Minnesota and Oregon. Cacti from Arizona prosper in any dry area. The idea is to use plants found in similar regions.

▬▬▬ EXAMPLES OF NATIVE PLANTS ▬▬▬

CLIMATIC CONDITIONS	PLANT CHARACTERISTICS	EXAMPLES
High altitudes	Withstand temperature extremes, wind and snow	Alpines
Little rainfall	Drought-tolerant	(see page 66)
Sandy soil	Prefer sandy soil	Yarrow, sedum
Seaside	Withstand salty winds	Rugosa roses
Damp, rainy	Grow in partial shade and tolerate damp conditions	Ferns, hosta

The Value of a Plant's Character

What characteristics do you look for in the plants you choose? Do you prefer a particular size and shape, a certain flower color, or productivity in food plants? As mentioned before, only the plants that suit your taste as well as your site, belong in your garden. But once you have decided your preferences for the more obvious qualities, consider some characteristics that will really save you money in the long-run.

Disease Resistance

Two rose bushes are next to each other in a border garden. One is practically defoliated, with the remaining leaves covered in black blotches. The other has full leaves and boasts blooms to boot. What makes the difference? Some plants are just naturally more resistant to disease than others are, and we don't always know why. Perhaps the cuticle, the waxy coating, on the leaves of the healthy rose bush is thicker, less acidic, or tougher than that of the sick rose bush. Physical and chemical attributes account for much of the mystique of natural resistance.

We may not know exactly *why* some plants resist illness, but we know disease resistance exists. Unfortunately, resistance often varies with climate or locale. Still, resistant varieties help you save money fighting plant diseases or replacing lost plants. Look for varieties that are resistant to diseases that are particularly prevalent in your area.

▰▰▰ RECOMMENDED DISEASE-RESISTANT VARIETIES ▰▰▰

Plant	Resistant Varieties
Fruit	
Hardy Kiwi	Issai
Raspberry	Many varieties
Strawberry	Allstar, Earliglow, Guardian, Surecrop
Wineberry	*Rubus phoenicolasius*
Vegetables	
Asparagus	Jersey Giant, Mary Washington
Bean (snap)	Derby, Greensleeves, Tendercrop, Top Crop
Bean (pole)	Kentucky Wonder
Bean (lima)	Eastland
Broccoli	Green Comet, Emperor hybrid
Corn	Burpee's Honeycross, Camelot (white)
Cucumber	Early Pride hybrid, Salad Bush hybrid, Sweet Success Amira hybrid
Eggplant	Vittoria hybrid
Melon	Ambrosia hybrid, Bush Charleston Gray, Ediato Muskmelon, Dixie Queen, Sweet'n Early hybrid, Sweet Dream hybrid, Sweet Favorite
Pea	Green Arrow, Maestro, Sugar Bon, Sugar Snap
Pepper	Golden Summer hybrid, Gypsy hybrid, Bell Boy, Lemon Bell
Potato	Kennebec
Pumpkin	Baby Bear
Spinach	Melody hybrid
Tomato**	Super Beefstake, Roma, Better Boy, Parks Whopper, Better Bush, Celebrity, Big Pick
Watermelon	Crimson Sweet

**Look for the symbols V, F, FF, N, T, A in the names of tomato varieties.

DISEASE-RESISTANT VARIETIES (CONTINUED)

PLANT	RESISTANT VARIETIES
Turfgrass*	
Bluegrass	A-34, Birka, Nugget, Sydsport
Fescues	Biljart, Highlight, Scaldis
Bentgrass	Northland, Waukanda
Ryegrass	Derby Ensporta

*For best disease resistance use a blend of three or more bluegrasses and fescues for lawns.

Trees	
Apple	Liberty, Priscilla, Prima
Chinese Chestnut	Dynham hybrids

Flowers	
Coreopsis	Early Sunrise
Geranium	Tetraploid hybrids
Marigold	Marvel hybrids
Nicotiana	All varieties
Roses	Rugosa species and hybrids
Zinnia	Star White

Don't assume that just because you bought certified disease-free plants or resistant varieties, your plants will never get sick. The rest is up to you. Just as you can keep susceptible plants healthy with proper care, disease-resistant plants can get sick if not maintained properly. (See Chapter 6 for more on how to keep plants in their prime.)

MONEY-SAVING TIP
Choose disease-resistant varieties for longer-lived plants.

Drought Resistance

Plants that evolved in arid places had to adapt in order to survive. Thin leaves, a glossy coating, fuzzy stems, or fleshy plant parts all help prevent water loss. Cacti are the classic example of drought resistance. But other plants also tolerate a lack of water. Remember that newly transplanted specimens usually will need to be kept moist until they adapt to their new surroundings.

▰▰▰ A SAMPLING OF DROUGHT-TOLERANT PLANTS ▰▰▰

ANNUALS	PERENNIALS	TREES/SHRUBS
Morning glory	Yarrow	Barberry
Portulaca	Ornamental grasses	Broom
	Rudbeckia	Cotoneasters
	Coreopsis	Goldenrain tree
	Gaillardia	Junipers
	Iris (non-bearded)	Locust
	Narcissus	Pea shrubs
	Sedum	Pines
	Verbena	Oaks
	Yucca	Red flowering quince
		Russian broom
		Russian olive
		Walnut
		Wild lilac

For more drought-tolerant varieties look under individual headings on pages 69–74.

Cold Hardiness

Frost damage can affect plants in many ways. Spring frosts may kill flowering buds, ruining a flowering or fruiting season, but causing little or no permanent damage. Severe winter cold may split branches or stems, which can kill the plant.

Gardeners who live in cold climate areas, including high elevations or northern latitudes, learn quickly to rely on short-season, late-blooming, and cold-hardy plants. If you garden in such an area, look for these designations when choosing varieties. Plants that evolved in cold climates developed some clever tricks for foiling frost. Short-season varieties take less time to flower or fruit than others of their type. They don't really tolerate cold, they avoid it. Late bloomers don't break bud in the spring until after hard frosts, hopefully. And cold-hardy perennials, shrubs, and trees have a unique method of surviving winter's chill, called super-cooling.

Cool temperatures alone don't cause winter damage. Dehydrating winds, bright sun, and temperature fluctuations all contribute to damage. Water retained in cells, freezing and swelling, and thawing and re-freezing causes structural damage to plants. Cells burst and irreparably damage tissues. Research has discovered cold-hardy plants suffer less damage because they evacuate water from their cells prior to going

COLD-TOLERANT PLANTS

VEGETABLES & FRUITS	FLOWERS	SHRUBS AND TREES
Carrots	Aster	Apple (most)
Kale	Bleeding heart	Cotoneaster
Parsnips	Columbine	Junipers
Raspberries	Coreopsis	Kordesii and rugosa
Rhubarb	Crocus	roses
Rutabagas	Daylilies	Late lilac
Salsify	Foxglove	Norway spruce
Turnips	Hardy geranium	Pear
	Hosta	Plum (some)
	Iris	Russian olive
	Phlox	Serviceberry
	Rudbeckias	Sour cherry
	Sedums	Staghorn sumac
	Tulips	'Minuet' weigela
	Yarrow	
	Yellow corydalis	

dormant, the process called super-cooling. If there is less water and less swelling, then less damage will occur.

Sun and Heat Tolerance

Severe cold as well as unrelenting heat, can damage plant tissues. With too much sun and heat, blossoms fade and fall, leaves drop, and fruit fails to develop. Even if plants are well-watered, the rate of transpiration (see Chapter 1) often outpaces the ability of the roots to absorb and replace lost moisture. But some plants have found ways to beat the heat.

Money-Saving Plant Varieties

Since many plants suitable for specific conditions have been discussed, let's consider those that perform well in a variety of garden settings. While there are bound to be exceptions, the plants listed in this section perform well all over the United States unless specifically noted.

Garden Vegetables

This may sound a little obvious, but grow what you like to eat. No matter how good a crop you turn out, it's a waste of time and money if no one eats it.

The second important consideration for a cost-effective plot is to grow only those crops which are cheaper to grow than buy. Why toil over a bed of spuds when you can buy 10 pounds for $1.59? Actually, there are a couple of sound exceptions to this rule. If your heart's desire is for a vegetable variety unavailable at the grocery store, grow your own. If you worry about an organic diet, grow your own. But if cost is a factor, leave the cheap vegetables to the truck farmers. For a more detailed assessment of how productive various vegetables are compared to the amount of row space and growing time they require, see Appendix A.

MONEY-SAVING TIP

Don't waste money and time growing crops that are cheaper to buy than grow.

SELECTED HEAT-TOLERANT PLANTS

VEGETABLES

- Beans
- Corn
- Cucumbers
- Melons
- Okra
- New Zealand spinach
- Swiss chard

FLOWERS

- Begonia cocktail hybrids
- Dusty miller
- Gerbera daisy
- Pinks
- Rudbeckia
- Yarrow
- Zinnia
- Ornamental grasses
- Blue fescue
- Pampas grass
- Bamboo

Herbs

Herbs are among the most trouble-free plants to grow, rarely bothered by pests or diseases. This is an endearing quality to the gardener who likes to save time and money. Most are attractive plants that add beauty to the landscape and many are exquisitely fragrant. They fit in anywhere; interplant into a border or grow in containers, a windowbox, or a pot on a sunny kitchen windowsill.

Look at some of the wonderful ways you can save money through the benefit of homegrown herbs. Grow gourmet cooking herbs such as Italian parsley or cilantro, that are often difficult to find in grocery stores. Common culinary herbs such as dill, oregano, sage, and tarragon transcend into gourmet delights when homegrown and just-picked fresh. Moreover, *all* herbs seem to taste better when you know you didn't have to pay the high prices they bring at the market. Grow mints, chamomile, and lemon balm, among others, to create your own soothing teas at a fraction the cost of store-bought. You can also dry herbs (see pages 141–143) to use and enjoy all through the year, or to give as gifts.

MONEY-SAVING VEGETABLE VARIETIES

VEGETABLE	VARIETIES
Asparagus	Jersey Giant*, Waltham
Beans (Bush)	Blue Lake*, Purple Tepee, Tendercrop*
Beans (Pole)	Kentucky Blue (AAS), Romano, Goldcrop Wax (AAS)*
Beans (Lima)	Fordhook (AAS)
Beans (Shelling)	Several (Generally store-bought are cheaper than homegrown)
Beets	Detroit Supreme (AAS), Early Wonder, Cylindra, Golden
Broccoli	Green Comet (AAS), Premium Crop (AAS)
Brussels Sprouts	Jade Cross hybrid
Cabbage	Derby Day*, Stonehead (AAS), Copenhagen Market, Late Flat Dutch, Red Acre
Chinese Cabbage	Green Rocket hybrid
Cauliflower	Snow Crown (AAS), Hybrid Snow King*, Ravella
Carrots	Nantes Slendero, Nantes Half Long, Royal Chantenay, Toudo hybrid, Thumbelina (AAS)
Celery	Golden Self-Blanching
Celeriac	Avari
Corn	Miracle, Silver Queen, Early Xtra-Sweet (AAS) SE type**, Burpee's Breeders, Choice, Honey 'N Pearl (AAS)
Cucumber	Fanfare (AAS)*, Salad Bush (AAS)*, Lemon Cuke, Northern Pickling
Eggplant	Dusty hybrid
Endive	Arugula
Garlic	Racomabole, Elephant
Jerusalem Artichoke	Various
Kohlrabi	Grand Duke (AAS)
Leek	King Richard, Giant Musselburgh
Lettuce	Buttercrunch, Grand Rapids, Oakleaf, Red Sails (AAS)
Melons	Sweet 'n Early, Sugar Baby, Hearts of Gold, Sweet Favorite (AAS)*

MONEY-SAVING VEGETABLE VARIETIES (CONTINUED)

VEGETABLE	VARIETY
Okra	Clemson Spineless (AAS)
Onions	Sweet Spanish types, Carmen (red)
Parsnips	All America
Peas	Maestro*, Oregon Sugar Pod, Sugar Bon*, Sugar Snap (AAS)*
Peppers (Sweet)	Gypsy (AAS)*, Crispy, Sweet Banana
Peppers (Hot)	Anaheim, Jalapeno
Potatoes	Purple Peruvian, Yellow Finns, Ordinary
Pumpkin	Baby Bear (AAS)*, Autumn Gold (AAS), Triple Treat
Radish	Cherry Belle, Easter Egg
Rhubarb	MacDonald, Canada Red
Rutabaga	Laurentian
Squash (Summer)	Zucchini, Yellow Crook-neck, Scallop, Sunburst (AAS)
Squash (Winter)	Acorn, Ebony, Butternut
Spinach	Bloomsdale, Longstanding, New Zealand
Swiss Chard	Large White Broad, Ribbed
Tomatoes	Sweet 100, Celebrity (AAS)*, Early Girl, Roma VF
Turnips	Purple-Top White, Globe, Tokyo Cross

AAS All-America Selections Winner; plants that have proven reliable in various conditions across the U.S.

* Disease resistant.
** SE, or Sugar Enhanced corn, is bred to mature much sweeter than "regular" sweet corn. It holds its flavor longer, both while still on the stalk, and later under refrigeration.

MONEY-SAVING HERBS

HERB	COST SAVINGS OF GROWING**	HERB	COST SAVINGS OF GROWING**
Basil	High	Parsley	Medium
Borage	High	Pennyroyal*	High
Chamomile	Medium	Rosemary*	High
Chives*	Medium	Sage*	High
Cilantro	High	Savory	High
Dill	Medium	Thyme*	High
Lemon balm	High	Tarragon*	High
Mints*	Medium		
Oregano*	High		

*Drought-resistant
** As compared to buying in store

Small Fruits

Berries and other small fruits add a touch of sweetness to the summer garden. While expensive in the supermarket, most small fruits are easy to grow. For a detailed list of recommended high-productivity fruit varieties, see Appendix B.

FRUIT PLANT PRODUCTION RATES

PLANT	POUNDS OF FRUIT PRODUCED PER PLANT
Blackberry	12–25
Blueberry	4–5
Currant	5–8
Elderberry	10–15
Gooseberry	8–10
Raspberry	2–4

Annual and Perennial Flowers

We appreciate flowers for their marvelous colors, textures and aromas. Annuals provide color all season, while gardeners wait patiently for perennial favorites. By blending the two types, you can create a lasting portrait in living color.

BEST-VALUE FLOWER CHOICES

Astilbe(P)
Bee balm(P)
Bellflower(P)
Black-eyed susan(P)
Bleeding heart(P)
California poppy(A)
Columbine(P)
Coral bells(P)
Coreopsis(P)
Cornflower(A,P)
Corydalis(P)
Cosmos(A)
Daylily(P)
Fall aster(P)

Foxglove(B)
Garden phlox(P)
Golden
  marguerite(P)
Hardy geranium(P)
Impatiens(A)
Michaelmas daisy(P)
Nasturtium(A)
Pansies(P)
Pelargonium(A)
Petunias(A)
Pinks(P)
Primroses(P)
Purple coneflower(P)

Shasta daisy(P)
Siberian iris(P)
Snapdragons(A)
Sneezeweed(P)
Sunflowers(A,P)
Tree mallow(P)
Windflower(P)

Turf and Ground Covers

Choices in ground covers have expanded wildly in the last few years. From play turf to low-maintenance 'Blue Carpet' juniper, there is something for every lifestyle and every pocketbook. As nice as a lawn is, consider the time and expense that goes into maintaining it, and alternatives become all the more attractive. Many tolerate drought much better than a lawn, which saves you money on watering. And most add visual interest to the landscape that turf can't touch. Those listed tend to spread readily to cover the area, another valuable characteristic.

BEST-VALUE GROUND COVER CHOICES

Bellflowers
Bishop's weed
Boston ivy
Bugleweed
Chamomile***
Cotoneaster**
Creeping mahonia
Creeping phlox**
Crownvetch**
Dichondra*/***
English ivy
Flowering bulbs (en masse)

Forget-me-nots
Gazania
Hen and chicks**
Irish moss
Juniper
New Zealand brass buttons
Ornamental grasses
Pachysandra
Portulaca
Prostrate rosemary
Rockcress
Rock rose

Roses (low growing and trailing varieties)
Sedum**
Silvervein creeper
Snow-in-summer
Sweet woodruff**
Thymes (many varieties)
Vinca
Virginia creeper
Wild ginger
Wintergreen
Zoysia*

* Not cold hardy
** Drought-tolerant once established
*** Tolerates foot traffic

Climbers and Vines

Climbers and vines add interest to spaces that might otherwise go bare. Use them to create a privacy screen or to obstruct an unpleasant view. Quick growing annuals are handy for a nearly instant solution to such landscape problems, while perennials provide long-term cover. Growing and training vines is easy. Direct seed or transplant annuals where you want them to grow, and provide a trellis or other support structure at planting time. Plant perennial vines as you would other perennials. The method differs somewhat for container plants and bare-

MONEY-SAVING TIP
Create a low-cost alternative to fancy fencing with a climbing vine planting.

root plants (see page 83, for transplanting instructions). Some useful suggestions follow.

BEST-VALUE CLIMBERS AND VINES

ANNUALS

Black-eyed susan
  vine
Morning glory
Scarlet runner bean
Sweet pea
Trailing nasturtium

PERENNIALS

Baugainvillea**
Bittersweet*
Clematis
Climbing hydrangea
Climbing roses
  (many varieties)
Fiveleaf akebia
Grapes

Hall's honeysuckle
  'halliana'
Ivies — Boston,
  English
Kolomikta kiwi
Silver lace vine
Trumpet vine
Virginia creeper
Wisteria

* Drought tolerant once established
** Not cold hardy

Landscape Shrubs

The main reason for landscape shrubs is to provide visual interest in the yard or garden. Those that stand out remain attractive even after their main growing season. Shrubs also provide a haven for birds.

BEST-VALUE LANDSCAPE SHRUBS

Arborvitae
Barberry**
Cotoneaster**
Forsythia
Hollies
Hydrangea

Juniper**
Lilac
Oregon grape
Potentilla
Rhododendron
Rose

Rose-of-sharon
Scotch broom
Spirea
Viburnums

** Drought tolerant once established

Shade and Landscape Trees

Few things in life are more rewarding than trees. They provide shade, privacy, and good company. Recommended types on the next page are low-maintenance, and offer at least two seasons of interest.

BEST-VALUE TREES

American sweet gum
Austrian pine
Bradford pear
Catalpa
Chokecherry
Crabapple
Deodor cedar
European hazelnut

Ginkgo
Golden raintree*
Juniper*
Kousa dogwood*
Maples
Mulberry*
Russian olive*
Serviceberry**

Staghorn sumac
Sargent flowering
  cherry
Viburnum
Washington Haw-
  thorn

*Drought tolerant once established
**Prefers acid soil

NOTE
Avoid the following trees: American elm, Box elder, Black walnut, Japanese angelica, Osage orange

5

SAVE FROM THE START

Plants that get the right start in life survive to thrive, giving you the best possible return for your dollar. They don't require extras, such as expensive grow lights. They simply have basic needs.

Seeds Equal Pennies

When buying plants, seeds are much cheaper than transplants. Compare two extremes. Tetraploid pelargoniums cost $2.95 for a packet of only five seeds, nearly 60¢ for each plant.

A transplant, however, costs around $3. Of course, you have to factor in the cost of growing the seed, but after doing that, even expensive seed is still a bargain. Then there are the seeds you buy on sale or wholesale, or those you save from your own plants. Outside of a few pennies for seed, soil, and water, the costs are negligible for a homegrown transplant.

Seeds Have Needs

Tucked away in its cozy little hiding place, protected by a tough seedcoat, a baby plant waits to make its grand entrance into the world. When conditions of light, temperature, and moisture are just right, which varies by the type of seed, the embryo bursts forth. It carries just enough nutrition in the seed for the incredible feat of breaking free and stretching upward. Afterwards, it makes its own food. Through the miraculous process of photosynthesis, plant cells convert light, air, water, and soil nutrients into sugars, starches, and proteins.

Seeds may be direct seeded, which means planted directly into the garden where they will grow, or started in containers for later transplanting. Most plants are better suited to one method than the other.

Direct Seeding

This is the original plan for seed-bearing plants. They flower, set seed, and some seeds manage to get a foothold. Some types of garden seeds, especially those that develop extensive root systems, are best suited to direct seeding.

PLANTS SUITABLE FOR DIRECT SEEDING

FLOWERS

Baby snapdragon
Borage
Blazing star
Blue thimble flower
Calendula
Cape forget-me-not
Celosia
Chinese forget-me-not
Chinese houses
Corn cockle
Cornflower
Cosmos
California poppy
Desert bluebells
Flanders field poppy
Flax

Godetia
Larkspur
Lupines
Lychnis
Marigold
Morning glory
Nasturtium
Portulaca
Summer forget-me-
  not
Toadflax
Virginian stock

VEGETABLES

Beans
Beets
Broccoli
Cabbage
Carrots
Cauliflower
Chard
Corn
Cucumber
Lettuce
Onion (sets)
Okra
Peas
Potatoes (spuds)
Pumpkin
Radish
Spinach
Squash
Turnip

Direct seeding begins with preparing a seed-bed. Begin by removing all weeds and cultivating the soil. Rent a rototiller or get a good work-out turning the soil by hand. Rake the soil to remove any clumps, sticks, or rocks, and break the soil into fine particles. Water the area the day before planting so the soil is moist. You may want to treat the soil with an insecticide, such as diazinon (one of the less toxic of the chemical insecticides) or diatomaceous earth (an organic alternative), especially in soil freshly turned from sod. If soil-dwelling insects such as armyworms or cutworms get your plants before they emerge, you not only waste the money, time, and effort of planting, but you fall behind in the growing season.

MONEY-SAVING TIP
Space seed plantings to avoid wasting seeds and having to pull out healthy plants later.

You can broadcast seeds or plant them in rows. Spice dispensers, such as those for salt substitutes, make handy, free seed broadcasters. Those with smaller holes work for small-seeded crops, such as carrots; those with larger holes, are great for bigger seeds, such as marigolds. Fill the dispenser and gently scatter the seeds evenly over the prepared area. Scatter tiny seeds more evenly by mixing with fine sand for a carrying medium. To plant in rows, use a dibble, made from a stick or your finger, to poke a hole the appropriate depth into the soil, and drop a seed or two in each hole. Use either method for raised beds or wide rows.

I include broadcast seeding because many gardeners use it, but I don't. I think it wastes seed. It *is* faster than placing each individual seed where it belongs. Much of the time saved is imaginary, because thinning the thickly sprouted seeds takes time. Since it is more difficult for me to justify yanking out a perfectly healthy seedling than it is to space my plantings in the first place, I take the extra few minutes spacing seeds according to their size at maturity. Since I plant wide rows in raised beds, I space the seeds a certain distance apart from a center

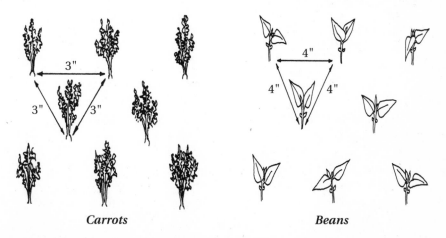

Carrots   *Beans*

Planting seeds at desired final plant spacing: carrot seeds 3 inches apart on all sides, bean seeds 4 inches apart.

point. For example, carrot seeds are 3 inches apart on all sides and bean seeds are 4-inches apart.

Once planted, cover seeds lightly with fine soil. The standard rule of thumb is cover seeds with soil two or three times as deep as the seed's thickness. Gently press on soil over the seeds until dirt is firm. Remember to keep moist. Tender seedlings will die if allowed to dry out.

When starting vining plants, such as pole beans, scarlet runner beans, or sweet peas, plant a support along with them.

Another prime candidate for direct seeding is a lawn. Till and amend the soil; most lawns benefit from tilling in peat moss or other organic matter. Rake until as even as possible, then compact with a roller, a large metal drum you rent and fill half-full with water for weight.

Seed evenly with a spreader by walking across the area first in one direction, then perpendicular to the first pattern, and finally at a diagonal. This pattern prevents bare spots.

The best germination depends on good seed, warm temperatures, and constant moisture. Until the grass is about 1 inch tall, water it every day. Spread a grass seed mulch over the seed to reduce water loss. You will save money substantially by planting your own lawn rather than laying sod or hiring someone else to install it either way.

Plant at the Right Temperature

It is important to know the temperature tolerance of the seeds you plant. Cool-season plants will sprout and grow at 40°F. Due to the process of microbial breakdown, however, cold soil has few organic nutrients available to plants. (See Chapter 6 for ways to jumpstart plants in the cold.) But warm-season plants will rot at 40°F. Most plants germinate very well at temperatures between 60° and 70°F.

COOL SEASON AND WARM SEASON CROPS

Cool Season Crops	Warm Season Crops
Broccoli	Corn
Peas	Melons
Onions	Beans
Spinach	Cucumbers
Carrots	Marigolds
Lettuce	Geraniums
Pansies	Begonias
Petunias	
Violets	

Planting Bulbs, Corms, and Tubers

Not all plants start best from seed. Many, such as tulips, gladiolus, and dahlias, propagate best from underground storage organs (as discussed in Chapter 3). The methods for planting bulbs, corms, and tubers are similar to planting seed, except bulbs used for naturalizing or planted in grass. In these cases, don't prepare the soil in advance, instead use a handy bulb planter for forming holes.

For perennials, use a hand trowel to dig holes about three times deeper than the width of the bulb. This insulates the bulbs from extreme temperatures. Irises are one exception. Plant them with part of the rhizome above ground. Planting irises too deeply will kill them. Likewise, plant onions and garlic with the tops nearly exposed.

It is absolutely critical to place bulbs, corms, and other underground storage organs in the soil with the growing tip facing the sky. If you are not sure which end is the growing tip, check for roots. The growing tip is on the opposite end. Dahlias and other tuberous plants should have small growing shoots coming out of the tuber. Plant them so the tips of the shoots point up. Make sure you don't break or damage growing tips.

▬ PLANTS SUITABLE FOR STARTING IN CONTAINERS ▬

FLOWERS

Ageratum	Godetia	
Anemone	Impatiens	
Aster	Lobelia	
Astilbe	Lupine	
Begonias	Marigold*	
Bleeding heart	Nicotiana	
Calendula*	Pansy	
Carnation	Petunia	
Celosia	Primrose	
Columbine	Portulaca	
Coneflower	Potentilla	
Delphinium	Salvia	
Dusty miller	Snapdragon*	
Pelargonium	Sweet alyssum*	
Gerbera daisy	Zinnia	

VEGETABLES

Broccoli
Cauliflower
Cantaloupe**
Cucumber**
Lettuce
Peppers
Squash**
Tomato
Watermelon**

* These plants reseed themselves.
** Always start in peat pots and transplant, pot and all, to avoid disturbing roots.

Sprinkle a little bone meal in the hole before placing the bulb to help the roots develop. Place the bulb in the hole, fill with the soil removed from it, and press down gently.

Start Your Own Seeds in Containers

You can start transplants either indoors in containers or in a cold frame (See page 82). Start them under controlled conditions to get a jump on the growing season. For gardeners in areas with short growing seasons, this is standard practice. Also, plants that originated in the tropics, such as tomatoes or peppers, require a long, warm growing season to ripen fruit. Start them as transplants.

Seed-Starting Supplies

Starting seeds in containers requires seeds, a growing medium, and containers. Quell that stingy urge to use garden soil in containers. As discussed in Chapter 1, it compacts and carries disease organisms to which seedlings may succumb. A bag of seed-starting medium is not a bad investment, or mix your own as described on pages 6–8.

The next consideration is the container. The only requirements for transplant containers is that they must be at least 2½ inches deep to allow for young, spreading roots, and they must have drainage holes. Those nicely matching plastic models at the garden center are a landfill nightmare. If you must buy them, use them carefully, wash thoroughly, and *re-use* them.

Do you need some suggestions to get started looking for free containers? Piece together wooden flats from scrap lumber, but make sure they are not painted or coated with a toxic preservative. Don't use old painted wood or treated lumber as it may contain toxins that could leach into the container soil. Cut milk cartons lengthwise and slice a few holes

 Cheap Trick for Starting Large Seeds

Try this method for starting large seeds that don't tolerate handling after they sprout, such as cucumber and melon.

→ Cut pieces of sod into 2-inch square chunks. (Make sure the turf has never been treated with an herbicide.)

→ Turn sod upside-down, and insert two or three seeds in each piece.

→ After seeds sprout, cull to the best seedling.

in the bottom for drainage. Large, wax-coated cereal boxes and styrofoam take-out containers are made to order. For a built-in greenhouse effect save plastic boxes from delis or bakeries. Poke holes in the bottom, fill, plant, and put the lid on. Wash out used margarine or yogurt cups and plastic trays from snack foods. Save toilet paper rolls, cut in half, arrange on a tray, and fill. Learn to find food-safe containers.

> **MONEY-SAVING TIP**
> Know the individual light requirements of seeds you're germinating so you don't lose seedlings.

If you start seeds indoors, scrounge up trays to place beneath the draining containers. A shallow box lined with plastic wrap, plastic container lids, or cookie trays will work in a pinch.

Temperature is critical to how many seeds germinate and develop. Room temperature, 65° to 70°F works well to germinate most plants. Heating mats or tape underneath the seed containers encourage roots to grow downward. Once plants sprout, however, remove the bottom heat as cooler temperatures produce sturdier plants.

Sow the seed as for direct seeding. Don't worry about spacing. As soon as the seedlings show two to four leaves, carefully lift by the leaves and transplant into individual containers. Never pick up tiny seedlings by the stem because they will crush easily.

Windowpanes or Grow Lights

The final consideration for starting seeds indoors is their individual light requirements. Most seeds germinate best in darkness, but some won't sprout without a little light. Knowing the light requirements of the seeds you sow prevents mysterious disappointments.

▬ PLANT GERMINATION LIGHT REQUIREMENTS ▬

GERMINATE BEST WITH LIGHT		GERMINATE BEST IN DARKNESS
Ageratum	Snapdragons	Bachelor's buttons
Begonia	Strawflowers	Calendula
Coleus	Sweet alyssum	Delphinium
Cosmos	Chrysanthemum	Nasturtium
Godetia	Columbine	Other poppies
Impatiens	Foxglove	Painted daisy
Lobelia	Gaillardia	Pansies
Nicotiana	Oriental poppy	Phlox
Petunia	Primroses	Sweetpea
Portulaca	Shasta daisy	Verbena

The light level is just as important after the seeds sprout. If grown at room temperature, they need supplemental light to prevent spindly growth. Plants grown on windowsills will do fine if the microclimate near the window is cool enough.

The alternative is to purchase cool-watt fluorescent lights. Sold as shop lights in 4- and 8-foot lengths, the lights are inexpensive and perfectly adequate for the task. They do not radiate the full sun spectrum, but unless you intend to hold seedlings until they flower, they won't need the full sun spectrum. The range of light waves from shop lights are just what seedlings need. Hang the lights within a few inches of the plants' tops, and adjust the lights as the seedlings grow.

Transplant for the Long-Run

Whether homegrown or store-bought, transplants represent an investment in time or cash. Unfortunately, the stress of transplanting can cause plants to go into temporary shock. Even though the plants eventually recover, they may suffer a permanent loss of growth and productivity, which means a permanent loss of value. Reduce transplant shock by following these guidelines.

Transplanting Bedding Plants

Bedding plants and other small plants are easy to establish in the garden. They are already growing and have an active root system. Plant them in the spring as soon as it is warm enough for the species (see table, page 67). But don't rush out with a new flat of plants, and stick them in the ground. First you must harden them off. Most bedding plants are grown under greenhouse conditions and are not yet ready to take on the real world. Here are four critical steps to success.

Hardening off. Toughen bedding plants first to stretch your plant dollars. Hardening off is a physical toughening of plant tissues. It takes only a few days and pays off in the survival rate and vigor of transplants. Whether bringing home plants from the garden center or preparing your homegrown transplants, this is a crucial step. Begin by placing the plants outside for about thirty minutes in a protected site, near a south wall for instance. Even a gentle breeze can seem like a howling gale to pampered plants. The next day increase the plants' time and exposure to the elements. Continue this routine for about a week.

Site preparation. While the plants are hardening off, prepare the site by removing all weeds, turning and amending the soil, and dusting with diazinon or diatomaceous earth to kill soil-dwelling bugs.

Transplanting. Transplant on an overcast day or in the late afternoon. Use a garden trowel to dig holes for the transplants 1 to 2 inches deeper than the roots of the plants. Sprinkle a little fertilizer or 1 inch of compost at the bottom of each hole. Refill the hole so that the transplant rests at the same depth it grew in the container. Gently loosen the transplant's roots, and place in the hole. Pat into place, and water. Epsom salts (magnesium sulfate) makes a cheap fertilizer substitute for tomato transplants.

Coddle transplants. Coddle the transplants for a few days even though they have been hardened off. They will suffer less shock and will grow more quickly. Water frequently, but don't drown them. If the weather is windy, give them a wind break by placing a board or bale of straw between them and the prevailing wind. If it gets too hot or sunny, rig a shade cloth over them. A good start will result in more robust and productive plants when they mature.

Transplanting Container or Root-Ball Plants

Container plants, similar to bedding plants, have their roots established in a growing medium. Unlike spring bedding plants though, it is best to transplant container plants when dormant.

Perennials. Grow them in containers or special beds in the garden. Transplant at any time, but spring and fall are preferable. Top-growth is slower at these times, yet roots are still developing. At this stage the plant has the greatest chance of establishing roots before going dormant for the winter.

Step 1: Dig a hole 1 to 2 inches deeper and wider than the plants' roots.

Step 2: Add fertilizer or compost to the bottom of the hole and cover it with loose soil.

Step 3: Place plant, fill the hole around the roots with soil, and water.

The fun part about planting perennials is planning where you will plant them. Try arranging extensive borders using just the plants you propagate yourself (or sneak in a few store-bought plants if you must).

Make sure you plant perennials at the proper depth. Transplant most perennials at the same level they grew in the container or the field, usually with the crown at soil level. Perennials that tend to rot at the base grow better if planted higher. Plants that require dampness near the crown, such as Solomon's Seal and hostas should be planted lower.

Prepare a perennial bed by tilling and amending the soil at least a few days before planting. Ideally, this is a job for the previous fall. This gives the soil time to settle and mellow. If adding to an existing planting, begin by digging a hole about twice as big around as the roots of the plant and a few inches deeper. As for bedding plants, you can sprinkle in a little fertilizer or compost in the bottom and cover with soil. Water the potted plant and gently slide it from the container without breaking any roots. Carefully loosen some of the root soil. Tease any roots that have begun to grow in circles free of the root ball. Set in place and remove; refill the hole if necessary to adjust the planting depth. Backfill with soil from the hole and water well. As with bedding plants, pay perennials a little special attention until the roots are established.

Vines or climbers. Transplant vines or climbers from containers the same way as perennials. It is usually best to transplant in the spring to give the plant a chance to establish.

Install a trellis when planting climbers, or place the new plant near an existing support, such as a fence or tree. Supports, while necessary for climbers, pose a few challenges. Supports shelter the growing plant from essential rain or sprinkler water. If you use another plant as a support, the two will compete for water and nutrients. Plant climbers at least 1 foot from a support to reduce water deflection and allow for adequate air circulation. But plant them nearer tree trunks, however, since competing feeder roots spread out near the drip line rather than near the trunk.

Plant climbers grafted to a rootstock, such as wisteria and climbing roses, with the graft union below the soil level. This protects the union from extreme temperatures, and prompts the climber to send out its own roots. Also, clematis develops more buds if set about 2 inches deeper than it originally grew.

Shrubs and Trees. These are sold in containers or with the roots wrapped in burlap. The method for transplanting shrubs and trees is similar to the method used for other container plants, but on a larger scale. For roots wrapped in burlap, treat as you would a container plant, unless the soil crumbles. In that case don't worry, just proceed as for a bare-root plant. (See next section.)

Place the plant in the ground. Without burying the plant any deeper, backfill about halfway and water well. Finish filling the hole, water again, and gently firm the soil down. Shovel a ring of soil around the drip line. This forms a water-retaining well that pools water and funnels it to the plant's roots. Remove the well before hard frost or during heavy rains.

Trees require an additional step. Many trees suffer root damage due to the effects of wind-rock. Winds rattle the tree, shaking it clear down to its unestablished roots. The motion tears tiny feeder roots, creates air pockets, and may prevent the tree from thriving. Place stakes or guy wires to keep the trunk in place while the roots gain strength. Don't make the common mistake of tying the tree down tightly. Tree roots need a little natural stress in order to grow strong. Make sure there is a little give in the tension of wires, or use a section of old rubber hose to tie the tree in place.

Transplanting Bare-Root Stock

Some of the best bargains in woody plants are bare-root plants. The selection is phenomenal, and it includes roses, grapes, blueberry bushes, canefruit, and many shrubs and trees.

Late winter is the best time to buy and plant. It is also the best time to dig up and move young plants that you have propagated yourself.

Plant bare-root plants as soon as you get them home, or dig them up, to prevent life-threatening dehydration. Bare-root plants are totally unprotected. If you cannot plant them immediately, place the plants in a bucket of water for no more than a few hours.

Check the plant carefully at both ends. Trim any damaged or spindly roots and cut back the top-growth in proportion to the roots. This seems to be a hard step for most gardeners, but the roots establish the life-blood of the plant and they must get top priority.

Prepare the soil the same as for container plants to transplant. Position the bare-root plant at the proper depth, again usually the same depth at which it grew previously. Build a cone of soil in the bottom of the hole and arrange the roots around it. Backfill, and water well.

Never Amend Backfill

Not only is it cheaper to use the original soil to backfill a planting hole, it is better for the plant. By digging a hole and filling it with amendments or foreign soil, you create an artificial environment with a dramatic interface between it and the surrounding native soil. The result is water does not flow freely between the two media, and plant roots become entrapped in the planting hole, much like they would in a container. At first, the plant will look normal, in fact, most plants will appear to thrive. After a while, the plant becomes virtually potbound and dies, leaving the conscientious backfiller to wonder why.

6

PLANT WELLNESS PAYS

Healthy plants are attractive and productive plants. They suffer less from pests and disease, and resist stress from heat, cold, wind, and drought. They make the best possible use of available water and nutrients. In short, healthy plants give you the most for your money.

Feeding Plants on a Budget

The most common mistake gardeners make is thinking more is better. If a bag of fertilizer says to apply a cup for every 10 feet of row, then two cups must make plants *really* grow. That is not the case. Manufacturer's instructions are not arbitrary numbers that somebody guessed at. Manufacturers base their instructions on the ability of plant roots to absorb nutrients in a set amount of time. This rate varies with the type, age, and health of the plant, as well as the soil type and texture.

Organic or Synthetic

A common misconception is that synthetic fertilizers are better than organic. Another misunderstanding is that organic is better than synthetic. You can make political or environmental arguments for synthetic or organic fertilizer, but the plants can't tell the difference as long as the nutrients are available. However, don't forget the many benefits of adding humus to your soil, which only organic amendments can supply.

Brand labels mean nothing to plants. It's the fertilizer analysis that counts — the list of three, sometimes four, numbers listed on the bag. They stand for the percentage of nitrogen (designated by the international chemical symbol N), phosphorus (P), potassium (K), and when present, sulfur (S), in the product, in that order. As mentioned in Chapter 1, these are the major elements plants need (except sulfur, which is a secondary element). Trace elements are also necessary, but manufacturers may or may not list them on labels. Organic fertilizers are much more likely to include these than manufacturers of chemical formulas.

Plants can only use nutrients that have been reduced to the molecular form. Chemical fertilizers work so fast because they have already been processed into the molecular form, whereas organic fertilizers must first be broken down by soil microbes. This activity depends on soil temperature. Below 70°F, soil microorganisms work slower, which makes the nutrients in organic fertilizer unavailable to plants in cold soils. Organic fertilizers release nutrients over a period of time, unlike synthetic fertilizers which make the nutrients available at time of application.

Chemical fertilizers dissolve fairly quickly in water, which makes them easily accessible to plants. Their labels instruct to water thoroughly after application. Unfortunately, this ready solubility also means that chemical fertilizers, unlike slow-release organics, leach more quickly from the soil.

For the best results with the least expense, strategically combine the two types of fertilizer. In the spring, while the soil is still cool, apply chemical fertilizer to lawn, flower borders, and vegetable gardens. Once the soil is warm, switch to compost or another low-cost organic source.

Organic fertilizers are not necessarily more costly than synthetics. This is commonly misstated, because the measurable amount of nitrogen, phosphorus, and potassium in synthetic fertilizers costs less per pound than those in many commercially prepared organic fertilizers. But those aren't the only sources of organic fertilizer. Once you know, roughly, the fertilizer analysis of organic compounds, which varies with different sources, you can mix your own fertilizers balanced for your particular needs, at a fraction of the cost. (See the next section for details.)

MONEY-SAVING TIP
Minimize fertilizer costs by using a carefully timed combination of chemical and organic mixtures.

This is where ingenuity and the willingness to scrounge for something pays off. I never buy fertilizer, and you don't have to either. So long as you supply the plants' nutrient requirements, it just doesn't matter to them where the nutrients come from, whether it is an organic or synthetic source. Refer back to Chapter 1 (page 11) for some cheap sources of soil amendments. Continue reading for instructions on how to make the best fertilizer money can't buy, compost.

How Much Fertilizer?

Most commercial fertilizers list application rates right on the bags. Follow these instructions and don't be tempted to fall into the trap of thinking more is better. Since nitrogen is the element lost most quickly from the soil, manufacturers often figure rates based on a plant's need for this essential nutrient.

Nitrogen Needed for Various Areas

AREA	NITROGEN NEEDED
Flower and Vegetable Gardens	1 pound/1000 square feet
Lawn	1 pound/1000 square feet
Landscape Shrubs and Trees	3 to 6 pounds*/1000 square feet

*Shrubs and trees use nitrogen at different rates depending on their size. Measure tree trunks 36 inches above the ground. If less than 6 inches in diameter, the tree will use from .15 to .3 pound of nitrogen for 1 inch of trunk diameter. If over 6 inches, apply at a rate of from .3 to .6 pound per inch of trunk diameter. Fertilize shrubs at the same rate as small trees or apply from .05 to .10 pound of nitrogen for 1 foot of height or spread of the plant.

If you purchase a product with a fertilizer analysis of 4–8–6, this means the product is 4 percent nitrogen. It takes 25 pounds of this product to yield 1 pound of actual nitrogen; 4 percent of 25 pounds is 1 pound.

Determine the pounds of product it takes to yield one pound of nitrogen with this formula:

Pounds of fertilizer product needed = 1 ÷ percent of nitrogen in product

MONEY-SAVING TIP
Mixing your own organic fertilizer costs less and allows you to tailor special compounds for particular plants.

After you figure how many pounds of a material it takes to supply a pound of nitrogen, find out how much nitrogen your garden needs. First determine the square footage of your garden by measuring the length of one side and one end, and multiplying the two numbers. For instance, a plot 50 feet by 20 feet is 1000 square feet of garden space. If your own is a 1000 square-foot garden, then you need 1 pound of nitrogen. If it's 2000 square feet, you need 2 pounds. But what if it's 748? Find out

FERTILIZERS:
COMPARATIVE ANALYSIS & NITROGEN CONTENT

As you can see from the following analysis, some products supply many times more nitrogen than others — and price has nothing to do with it. Urea is one of the cheapest products listed, yet supplies the most nitrogen.

PRODUCT NAME	N, P, K ANALYSIS	POUNDS OF PRODUCT TO SUPPLY 1 POUND N
All-Organic Plant Food	5–3–1	20
Ammonium Nitrate	33–0–0	3
Ammonium Sulfate	21–0–0	5
Blood Meal	15–1.3–.7	8.3
Bone Meal (raw)	4–21–.2	33
Chicken Manure	3–2–2	33
Compost (varies)	.5–.3–.8	200
Hoof and Horn Meal	14–2–0	7
Lilly Miller Tomato & Vegetable Food	4–8–6	25
Mushroom Compost	.7–.3–.3	143
Ortho Tomato & Vegetable Food	6–18–6	16
Seaweed Meal	2.8–.2–2.5	36
Steer Manure	.7–.7–.7	143
Superphosphate	0–18–0	0
Ultra Green Lawn Fertilizer	24–2–5	4
Urea	44–0–0	2.5
Wood Ashes	0–1–4.3	0

how many pounds of product you need for your plot with the following equation:

Pounds of product needed for your garden $=$ Pounds of product to supply 1 pound of nitrogen $\times$ the square feet of garden $\div$ by 1000

For our example this figures as follows:

25 × 748/1000 = 25 × .748 = 18.7 pounds of product for your garden

If math isn't your forté believe me I understand. The whole purpose for learning how to figure fertilizer rates is to avoid using too much and thereby wasting it. Besides the cost of the product, there are other consequences to consider if you overuse fertilizer. Most serious is the contamination of ground water by fertilizer runoff. You may not think the little bit of chemical that runs off your yard amounts to much, but

▬ TAILOR-MAKE FERTILIZER TO FIT YOUR PLANTS' NEEDS ▬

	PLANT GROUP			
	Beans, beets, carrots, corn, lettuce, radish, spinach, tomato	Cabbage, cauliflower, celery, kale, onions, parsley, peas, turnips	Asparagus	Cucumbers, melons, pumpkins, rhubarb, roses, squash
N–P–K Requirements	2–4–5	3–4–3	1–6–6	5–10–5
Bloodmeal (15–11.3–.7)	.7 pounds	1.6 pounds	0	1.2 pounds
Bone Meal (4–21–.2)	1 pound	2 pounds	1.4 pounds	2.4 pounds
Wood Ashes (0–1–4.3)	8.3 pounds	6.8 pounds	8.6 pounds	6.4 pounds
Total Pounds	10	10	10	10

multiply that by your neighbor's yard, and the entire neighborhood, your city, and beyond. The magnitude of the problem begins to come into focus.

Fertilize Frugally

The method of application depends on the type of fertilizer. Sprinkle granules around the base of plants, scratch into the soil, and water thoroughly to dissolve. Shovel a layer of compost or manure over the soil at the base of the plants, and scratch in with a hoe. This method is called side-dressing.

You can apply some fertilizers, including compost and manure, in liquid solution. Apply liquid fertilizers either to the soil or leaves. This is called foliar feeding. Plants can absorb nutrients in solution through their leaves as well as their roots. In fact, they absorb them more quickly this way. Apply these products through a sprayer or dissolve in a watering can and apply by hand. The second option is cheaper, but takes longer.

Is it possible, you may ask, to apply compost or manure as a liquid? The answer is, yes, if you brew a batch of fabulous, free "tea." Scoop

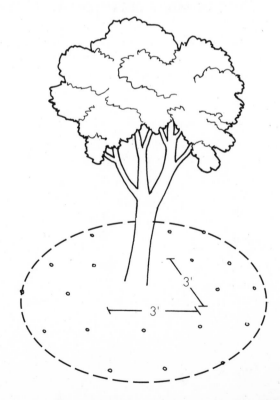

To fertilize landscape plants growing on a lawn, punch holes with a soil prober or an auger attached to an electric drill (see above), extending just beyond the dripline. Then put fertilizer in each hole.

some compost or manure into a bag — try using an old pillowcase, old pantyhose, gunnysack, flour sack, or any bag made of porous fabric. Tie off the top and set in a 5-gallon bucket. Use larger containers if you need more fertilizer. Fill the bucket with water to the top of the bag and let it sit for a day or two. Nutrients from the compost or manure leach into the water, which you then use to water your garden or to foliar feed.

For lawns, a spreader broadcasts fertilizer evenly over the surface of the grass, liquid fertilizer applicators that attach to your hose are also available. Either one is a fair investment. Fertilize woody landscape plants by broadcasting the product throughout the lawn and just outside the drip line. If landscape plants are growing through the lawn, however, punch holes with a soil probe or soil auger attached to an electric drill, and put the fertilizer into the holes. This prevents burning the grass with an overdose of nitrogen. Make the holes 1 to 2 inches across and about 8 inches deep, spaced about 2 feet apart. Avoid placing them close to tree trunks as this process could damage roots.

Save the Most — Compost!

Composting is one of the many small miracles that takes place in our gardens. It is the process by which weeds, garden debris, and other organic matter breaks down into dark, rich, crumbly soil, turning trash into treasure. The process occurs naturally without our help, but we can encourage it by controlling the circumstances under which it happens.

Why Compost?

Let's answer this question not only from a frugal point of view, but from that of plant health and a healthy global environment as well. Yard and garden waste account for 17 percent of the trash that finds its way into our landfills. Kitchen waste makes up another 8 percent. Combined, kitchen and garden waste account for one quarter of all the garbage we throw out. By composting, you save money used to dispose of waste, including bags and cans, as well as your time spent collecting it. And the environment also wins. You also get the world's best free fertilizer, compost. Not a bad return.

What makes compost so great? It is very rich in nutrients derived from plant and animal matter. Unlike many store-bought soil amendments, it contains trace elements. Compost is rich in humus, and you remember that great stuff.

The process of composting helps purify the end result by killing many seeds and harmful organisms present in the raw ingredients. It's the closest thing gardeners have to spinning straw (and weeds and manure and eggshells and more!) into gold.

What Does It Take to Make Compost?

The good news is that anybody can make compost. Actually, compost will make itself *without anybody.* Consider a maple tree near a fence line. Each year it sheds its leaves, and some of those leaves are blown against the fence where they pile up. In time, the bottom layer of those leaves is no longer recognizable as leaves, but transformed into a dark, sweet-smelling, crumbly soil.

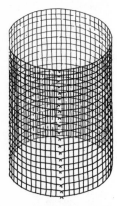

An easy homemade compost bin made of hardware cloth.

All organic matter rots. You can speed up the process by combining different types of matter, ventilating the mix to add oxygen, and keeping it moist. When you control the circumstances, the process speeds up considerably. You can make compost in weeks, not years.

In terms of composting, gardeners consider organic matter primarily a carbon-based material or a nitrogen-based material. Microbes burn approximately one part of nitrogen for every twenty-five parts of carbon they digest. So you need at least one part of nitrogen material for every twenty-five parts of carbon material. More nitrogen material is fine if you have it. Materials high in nitrogen, such as alfalfa meal, blood meal, or urea, act as pile activators by jump-starting the microbes into action.

COMPOST COMPONENTS

NITROGEN-BASED GREEN	CARBON-BASED BROWN
Alfalfa	Straw
Grass clippings	Leaves
Green weeds	Sawdust
Manures	Peanut hulls
Coffee grounds	Cocoa hulls
Seaweed	Hay
Milfoil (lake weeds)	Peat moss
Stalks, stems, and leaves from crops	Last year's mulch

Which materials are nitrogen and which are carbon? In general the easiest way to tell is that materials higher in nitrogen are green and those higher in carbon are brown.

Other ingredients add phosphorus, potassium, and trace minerals. Egg shells, wood ashes, banana skins, melon rinds, orange peels, stale bread, apple peels, potato skins, pea pods, and tea leaves are great for composting.

There are a few things that, although they are organic matter, do not belong in a garden compost pile. Leave the following out of the compost pile:

→ Weeds that have gone to seed. The seeds may survive.
→ Obviously diseased or insect-infested material.
→ Any meat, grease, or fat. It stinks and attracts vermin.
→ Cat and dog feces, which may transfer parasites to the garden.
→ Grass clippings or weeds that have been treated with weed killers. Chemicals may persist and poison the garden.
→ Pine needles or large branches. They don't harm the pile but take years to decompose.

Ready, Set, Compost!

You can make composting as easy and cheap as that leaf-dropping tree. All you need are the ingredients and as much time as you are willing to devote to the project.

For the sake of appearances, or ease of handling, you may wish to enclose the pile in a bin. My favorite siding for this job is a 10- to 12½-foot length of 48-inch-wide hardware cloth, ½- by 1-inch mesh. It is sturdy enough to be freestanding, forms a circle of perfect dimensions for composting, and won't leak any small pieces of the pile. Bend over a few of the wires on one edge to form hooks to attach it to the other edge in a cylinder. It's cheap, easy to use, lasts forever, and stores almost anywhere. Lumber scraps and chicken wire, salvaged concrete blocks, or bales of straw arranged together will also serve the purpose.

The dimensions of the pile affect how quickly it breaks down. Research has determined that the pile must be at least 3 feet high by 3 feet across in order to have enough mass to retain the heat generated in composting. As the microbes work, temperatures can reach 140°F inside the pile. These high temperatures kill weed seeds and disease organisms. Piles about 4 feet by 4 feet will work fine, but piles much larger than 5 feet around take a lot of work to keep actively composting. Larger piles require constant turning to keep oxygen supplied to those busy microbes.

There are no hard and fast rules for building a compost pile. Gardeners generally recommend layering nitrogen materials and carbon materials with a bit of soil, with finished compost or activator sprinkled throughout the pile as it is built. The first time you turn the pile this neat arrangement is shot. The most convenient way to compost is to toss in whatever is available at the moment. Weeds go in when you pull them, soil, and all. Toss in eggshells, coffee grounds, and melon rinds after breakfast. Throw cornstalks on the pile at the end of summer.

You can add many items whole to the compost pile, and they will degrade fine. But larger items, such as cornstalks, hedge trimmings, and spent broccoli plants, will break down much more quickly if chopped into smaller pieces first. When they are cut into pieces there is much more surface area on which the microbes can work. Reduce large pieces by running over a shallow pile of them with a lawn mower, hacking with an ax, or throwing them in a chipper/shredder.

Keep the pile moist as you add materials to it. An occasional sprinkling with the garden hose provides the microbes with water they need to survive. Don't let piles get dripping wet, however, as precious plant nutrients will leach out. Cover your pile during rainy weather or if it is within sprinkler range.

Turning the pile provides aerobic conditions for you and the pile. You get the exercise, and the pile gets a fresh supply of oxygen for those hard-working microbes. If using a bin, disassemble it, grab a fork, and start working. Turn the outsides of the old pile into the center so they will be exposed to microbial action. Sprinkle the pile with water intermittently as you turn it. The more frequently you turn the pile, the more quickly the compost will decompose.

Compost Companions

Many gardeners buy compost starters to get a pile fired up. These are basically high-nitrogen products that may or may not work, depending on what else is in your pile. Fresh green weeds, with a little soil clinging to their roots, or a shovelful of soil or compost, tossed at intervals into the pile will suffice. But for a great, cheap pile activator, try alfalfa. Toss in handfuls from bales (old or rained-on bales are the cheapest) or use an alfalfa meal product. Horse feed, rabbit food pellets, even some brands of cat litter, are almost pure alfalfa meal.

Pets, except dogs and cats, can contribute significantly to the nitrogen content of a compost pile, some will even do the work of turning for you. If you live in an area where it is possible, and you like animals, keep a pet rabbit or some chickens. Rabbit waste, collected in a bucket beneath the hutch, is high in nitrogen, a fact attested to by the urea odor. But emptied routinely into the compost pile, you avoid the odor, while adding its riches to the pile.

Chickens are even better than bunnies. Toss your compost materials into an enclosed chicken run and let them turn it all into a homogenized, highly nutritious blend. Every few weeks rake out the run and add to the compost pile. Chickens will also produce fresh eggs for breakfast, and they love to eat garden bugs!

Prevent Pests and Disease

Many pesticide labels advise to spray at the first sign of a problem, which is good advice. Early, consistent spray schedules help control pests and diseases. Even better and cheaper advice is to take steps to prevent such problems in the first place.

A Healthy Environment

So much of the information already discussed contributes to your plants' overall health. The best site, proper planting, and transplanting, using resistant varieties, adequate watering, drainage, and nutritional support all help keep plants in optimum condition. Healthy plants have an edge. They are less susceptible to physical stress, attack by disease, or infestation of pests. In fact, studies show insects recognize and prefer ailing plants.

The best way to manage your garden is to keep a watchful eye on plants. Take time to notice any which may be particularly susceptible to problems. Watch for puddling after rain — this signals poor drainage which could suffocate roots. Look for unusual growth patterns, spots on leaves or stems, curling leaves, or anything that looks out of the ordinary. Glance around the plants for any evidence of pests, but realize that unless they are causing actual damage you may not need to take any action.

MONEY-SAVING TIP
Keep a watchful eye out for signs of insect or disease damage so you can take prevention and control steps early and save more plants.

Make sure plants are not overcrowded; occasionally thin or divide them as necessary. This is especially important for good air circulation around perennials and shrubs. Damp, stagnant air trapped near foliage often leads to disease.

Pruning (discussed on pages 114–118) is important for good air movement.

Weed Out the Competition

The first line of defense is to kick the competition when it's down. Don't allow weeds to get a foothold. Not only are they unsightly, weeds are real enemies of any gardener. They rob the soil of water and nutrients meant for cultivated plants. Many harbor diseases or serve as alternate hosts for pests. If allowed to grow, they may shade plants from sunlight, block air circulation around foliage, or crowd out crops entirely.

Rather than battle established weeds and the problems they create, get them before they get you. One tactic is to spray a pre-emergent herbicide, which kills weeds *before* they emerge. Another weed combatant is a heavy, water-permeable fabric that acts as a weed mat, laid out between landscape plants. It physically blocks weeds from sprouting. It's not cheap, but the time and money you save over other forms of fighting weeds may make it a good choice for your garden. A similar tactic is to put down a thick layer of mulch (see page 109, Chapter 7).

Young weeds are easy to scrape away with a hoe. Cultivate carefully around tender, young plants to avoid damaging roots. Use a scuffle hoe or toothed-wheeled weeder to tear out weeds while they are still small. When all else fails, get down on your knees and yank up weeds by their roots. It's good exercise and a well-weeded patch leaves any gardener with a real sense of accomplishment.

Integrate and Interplant

It is the nature of disease organisms and pests to take the easiest route. What could be easier than moving down a row of your favorite host plants and attacking one after the other of them? Organic gardeners have known for generations a way to confound many pests, especially those that prefer one particular crop over others, and it doesn't cost a cent.

Interplanting — mixing and mingling different species of plants in a garden border — effectively confounds many types of pests. It slows the progression of diseases when the plant next to an infected one is not susceptible to the disease-causing organism. For pests, the turbulent scene of mixed textures, colors, and odors, jams their plant-seeking radar.

Rotate Crops

Many diseases and soilborne insects that attack plants remain in the soil even after you harvest the crop. They wait there to reinfest susceptible plants. If you plant the same crop or a closely related one in that site a disease or insect will probably attack the new planting. Prevent this needless loss by rotating your crops each year. The practice costs nothing and could save a lot.

Crop rotation requires only a little planning. If you plant tomatoes in one bed this year, then don't plant tomatoes or a related crop (see table) in the same bed for the next two years. If possible, it is best to let at least three years pass before planting where the same or related crop grew before.

Bar Bugs

One of the best methods to prevent insect damage is physically preventing bugs from touching plants. Several methods work well depending on the plant and the insect. All methods mentioned are very effective and reasonably inexpensive when done properly.

RELATED CROPS
FOR PLANNING A ROTATION SCHEDULE

SOLANECE AND ROOT CROPS

Eggplant
Peppers
Potatoes
Tomatoes
Celery
Beets
Carrots
Sweet potatoes
Parsnips
Salsify

LEGUMES

Beans
Peas
Okra

BRASSICAS

Broccoli
Brussels sprouts
Cabbage
Cauliflower
Kale
Bok choi
Chinese cabbage
Kohlrabi
Rutabaga
Turnip
Radish

ALLIUMS

Onions
Garlic
Leaks

OTHER

Sweet corn
Squash

Row covers are sheets of spun-bonded polypropylene that can be draped over food crops to eliminate insect problems. They are lightweight enough to drop directly onto most crops, or you can create a frame for the covering by bending PVC pipe or bamboo sticks. (Cheap tip: You can even grow useful bamboo stakes yourself.) The fabric stands between the bug and its meal. It allows most available sunlight and water to pass through freely and protects from wind, hail, slight frost, and windborne weed seeds, as well as bugs, birds, and small animals.

It is critical to cover the crops early, before bugs get to them, which is when planting or transplanting them. A sprinkling of inexpensive diazinon or diatomaceous earth raked into the soil will kill any current soil-dwelling inhabitants. This is important for direct seeded melons, a special favorite of cutworms. Leave enough slack in the fabric to allow for the eventual growth of the plants, and anchor the fabric along the edges with dirt or planks. This is very important, because not only might it blow away but also the idea is to prevent bugs from getting to the plant, and they crawl through the smallest spaces. Lift the cover occasionally to monitor a plant's progress.

Covers are most convenient for plants that will not flower for harvest, such as carrots or broccoli. Covers will work for plants that flower, such as cucumbers, as long as you remove the covers in time for pollination to occur.

Treat these fabric covers with respect to get your money's worth. Work cautiously around them, a careless swing of the hoe will tear the fabric. Never walk on them, always go around. Don't drive stakes through them as anchors. Fabric anchored by stakes will not always keep out bugs anyway, and the stakes will cause rips. Cut the fabric down to a size you can handle easily. You will run less risk of damaging the fabric while you are working with it. Above all else, fold or roll up fabric covers at the end of the season and store them. Don't just drop them in a pile on the floor of the garden shed, since mice find them irresistible for winter housing.

MONEY-SAVING TIP
Create effective cutworm collars from old plastic drinking straws.

Stem collars protect tender transplants from cutworm damage. Cutworms are underground caterpillar-like bugs. They will devastate beans, broccoli, cantaloupe, and a vast array of other plants with equal zeal. They are especially prevalent in new gardens freshly dug from sod or areas filled with weeds. A dash of diazinon or diatomaceous earth will eliminate those present at application. But for continuing and organic protection, use a stem collar. Stiff paper or cardboard are often recommended, but one of the best and cheapest substitutes I have found is a plastic drinking straw. Salvage used straws, and cut them into 1½-inch long pieces. Slit the pieces up one side, pull the plastic apart and fit around the stem of each transplant. Push the plastic down into the soil, and you have a plastic barrier no cutworm can chomp or climb.

Use Pesticides Conservatively

Sometimes a barrier isn't the answer. You wouldn't want to drape a cover over a rose bush or shimmy up an apple tree with a bolt of cheesecloth. There are situations when you need to spray a pesticide.

Many plants look or produce much better if kept on a regular spray schedule. Fruit trees in particular yield more fruit if maintained this way. This should be an important consideration in the decision to plant home fruit trees.

What you spray depends on several factors, one of which is your budget. Chemical pesticides are expensive in more ways than one. Research has determined toxins, once commonly used in the garden, can cause a range of ills from birth defects to cancers. Accidental ingestion by pets and children occurs every year, with tragic results. Toxins also wipe out beneficial insects, such as bees and ladybugs. And misapplication of chemical pesticides often results in plant damage.

As with the misuse of chemical fertilizers, the biggest problem home gardeners have with pesticides is over-application. Always follow label instructions to the letter. These are not mere recommendations, they

 When to Consult a Professional

Sometimes pest control is not a do-it-yourself project. For gardeners lucky enough to have large shade trees, and unlucky enough for those trees to become infested or diseased, consult a professional. The problem with trying to spray a large tree yourself is that its sheer size often makes for an ineffective application. Without proper equipment you simply cannot get adequate coverage, and without adequate coverage you are wasting your money. Always check professional's credentials and ask for references.

are law — it is illegal to misuse pesticides.

Each product lists what insects it is effective against and on which plants it is safe to use. A general pesticide with a wide range of applications, such as Orthene or diazinon, will handle most problems of home gardeners.

Organic pesticides, such as botanically derived rotenone, pyrethrum, ryania, and sabadilla are good substitutes for environmentally concerned gardeners. They pose less threat of environmental damage because they break down quickly, and will not leave any long-term residues. Other examples of non-toxic pesticides are horticultural oil sprays that coat and suffocate small bugs such as scale, and diatomaceous earth, which kills bugs at or beneath ground level when worked into the soil. Many organic pesticides, unfortunately, kill indiscriminately, wiping out pests and beneficial organisms alike.

Some of the most promising pest-control products are ones that cause disease — generating pest-specific disease organisms that spring to life like sea monkeys when mixed with water. They only harm the bug for which they are intended. Some examples include several forms of the bacteria *Bacillus thuringiensis* (Bt), marketed under various brand names and effective at battling caterpillars and Colorado potato beetles; *Nosema locustae,* sold as Grasshopper Attack, which is a grasshopper disease that prevents successive generations; and *Bacillus popilliae,* or milky spore disease, that wipes out Japanese beetles.

Homemade Insect Controls

Commercial pesticides can be expensive, and they are not always necessary. You can make effective substitutes for a spray at home very

Disposing of Pesticides

Many states set up regular hazardous waste pick-up stations at designated times and places. Always dispose of unused pesticides, as well as paints, solvents, and other chemicals, at designated stations. Most disposal sites provide an exchange service on site. If you need a pesticide or other chemical, you can pick up someone else's castoff for free. Contact your local state department that handles hazardous waste disposal for details of procedures in your area.

inexpensively. Try some of the following time-tested recipes on your garden:

→ **Soap spray** is one of the best combatants against aphids and other soft-bodied pests. Mix about 3 tablespoons of a mild laundry soap, such as Ivory Snow, with 1 gallon or water, and spray on both sides of leaves.

→ **Tobacco tea** is another effective homemade brew. Collect enough cigarette butts to fill a 1-pound coffee can. Place cigarette butts in a cloth bag, and steep in 3 to 4 gallons of water for a few days. This spray is highly effective against aphids, thrips, and leaf hoppers, a testimony to the toxicity of nicotine.

→ **Pyrethrin** is a botanical insecticide you can make if you grow the daisy-like flower *Chrysanthemum cinerariaefolium*. This spray packs a potent poison. Pour boiling water over the petals and spray as soon as the concoction cools.

→ **Hot pepper and garlic sprays** that combine the active ingredient capsicum, from pureed hot peppers, and sulfur compounds, from garlic, are highly effective against many types of insects, including the adult moth or butterfly forms of many species. Combine cayenne or other hot peppers, a few cloves of garlic, and a teaspoon of dishwashing liquid for stickiness. Mix ingredients in a blender until pureed. Strain and dilute with water.

→ **Bug spray** is a favorite of some organic gardeners. Collect a quantity of the offending bugs, and liquefy them in an old blender, reserved for this purpose. Strain, dilute, and spray.

How do you tell if you need to spray? Good advice to any gardener is to make sure there is actual damage before embarking on a control program. Many insects cohabitate peacefully with your plot, and never damage anything.

When insect controls are necessary, you will find some of the very best methods are free. Hand-picking insects, a fun hobby in its own right, is very effective at controlling populations of larger insects such as tomato hornworms, Colorado potato beetles, and cucumber beetles. Pop them into a bucket of soapy water or water mixed with kerosene, or toss them as a treat to pet chickens.

Encourage Beneficial Organisms

The use of beneficial organisms in the home garden is hardly new. If you think of Adam and Eve as the original garden pests, look at the effectiveness of one snake. Actually, snakes are wonderful, free rodenticides. They patrol for ground-level mice, shrews, bugs, and slugs. In return they need an accessible water source, maybe a nice, flat rock on which to sun themselves, and not to be run over by a lawn mower.

 **Bats** are another fine addition to any garden. Bats consume many times their own weight of flying insects over the course of the gardening season. Persuade them to roost near your garden by putting in a little bat condo. Commercially made bat houses are available, or construct one yourself.

Birds are valuable bug-eaters. They will reward your thoughtfulness with years of dedicated service. Provide them with a bird bath, some cover in the form of bushes or trees, a small house or two, and perhaps a free meal every now and then.

 Toads are underappreciated assets in the garden; they guzzle bugs daily. Encourage their presence with a damp, shady spot for them to hide in during hot, dry weather. A board propped up over a puddle is toad heaven.

 Predatory and parasitic insects prey on other bugs for free, and unless you garden in a vacuum, they usually come with the garden. Be careful not to annihilate them with broad-spectrum chemical pesticides.

Beneficial organisms, from barely visible mites to 6-inch-tall praying mantises, are available to work in your garden. You can purchase them, but your money would be better spent encouraging existing, native populations. The trouble with many store-bought bugs is they are disloyal, and will probably leave.

Plant flowering herbs, such as thymes, mints, rosemary, sage, and dill for beneficial adult insects to eat. Or entice them by interplanting your crops with daisies, petunias, cosmos, nasturtiums, marigolds, and sunflowers. Provide a water source. The lingering dew on plant leaves is often sufficient; the constant moisture provided by drip irrigation is ideal. Most important, don't spray pesticides. Welcome the beneficials that occur naturally in your garden.

COMMON BENEFICIAL INSECTS AND THEIR PREY

INSECT	ACTIVE FORM	PREY
Ladybug	Larva and adult	Aphids
Green lacewing	Larva	Aphids, mealybugs
Praying mantis	Nymph and adult	Caterpillars
Big-eyed bug	Adult	Various
Soldier bug	Adult	Various
Pirate bug	Adult	Various
Assassin bug	Adult	Various
Ambush bug	Adult	Various
Ground beetles	Adult	Soil dwellers
Parasitic wasps	Larvae and adult	Colorado potato beetle, tomato hornworm
Encarsia formosa	Larvae and adult	Whitefly
*Nosema locustae**	Spores	Grasshopper
Predatory mite*	Adult	Spider mite and whitefly
Spiders*	Juveniles, adults	Various
Tachinid fly	Larvae, adults	Caterpillars

*Not insects, but still useful pest control organisms.

Protect Against Birds

For the most part birds are very beneficial to the garden. They are wonderful insect predators, especially in the spring when they need a supply of protein to feed their young. But hungry birds also can take a toll on freshly sown seeds, tender seedlings and luscious fruits and berries. You may need one or more of the following controls:

→ **Netting** is an important barrier to birds and some small animals. It is an absolute necessity with expensive berry crops, such as blueberries and strawberries. To keep greedy beaks away from berries, support netting on a framework several inches from the plants. Peeled poles or scrap lumber make inexpensive, rustic-looking frames. Handled carefully, netting will last indefinitely.

→ **Plastic berry baskets, panty hose, cheesecloth, salvaged window screening,** and other no-cost finds also work to create handy bird deterrents. Fasten any of these to a wire tomato cage for an individual plant protector.

→ **Wire or fishing line,** stretched between row markers over newly planted seeds, makes an inexpensive bird repellent. As birds approach for a landing they are snagged by the unseen lines and quickly retreat to safer ground.

→ **Scarecrows** are cute but ineffective. Don't spend a cent on one.

Keep Critters Out

Your garden is no place for critters. You may enjoy a leisurely stroll with the family cat, but you won't be amused with his leavings. Dogs can trample a seed-bed faster than anything short of the neighbor's children, especially if you are out walking with the cat. Wild animals from deer to raccoon can do even more damage, because they are intentionally after your produce.

The most effective way to keep wayward wildlife from your garden is to erect a fence. Fencing materials are certainly not cheap, but a well-constructed fence will serve for years. Woven wire, poultry netting, or welded wire will keep out most neighborhood pets and pests. The bottom of the wire should be buried below soil level if rabbits are a problem. Foil persistent gophers by lining planting beds with fine mesh fencing. A fence up to 8 feet high is necessary to prevent deer from jumping over. Leave approximately the top 18 inches of the wire unattached to any support. This wobbly fence discourages such climbing critters as raccoon, porcupine, and opossum.

In lieu of expensive fencing you may first want to try some of the many intriguing animal repellents available. Forget the store-bought solutions and whip up your own thrifty alternatives. Here are a few suggestions:

→ **Hair clippings** from the local barbershop scattered around the garden scare off critters that fear the ominous odor of humans. A few articles of *really smelly* dirty laundry, left about the garden at night will also deter many wild animals, including deer, raccoons, and rabbits.

→ **A sulfurous odor** can be created by cracking a few eggs and letting set until pungent. The strong scent repels deer.

→ **Dried blood meal** scattered around plants keeps away deer, ground squirrels, rabbits, raccoons, and woodchucks.

→ **Hot peppers, garlic, vinegar,** and water mixed with a squirt of dishsoap and pureed in a blender deters large nibblers as well as insect pests from tasting any garden fare on which it has been sprayed.

➜ **Ammonia.** Ironically, the nasty smell of rags soaked in ammonia repels skunks and rats.

➜ **Beer.** Set out a shallow tray of beer to lure and drown slugs. To be truly frugal, use cheap beer.

➜ **Repellent plants.** Gopher spurge, *(Euphorbia lathyrus)* repels gophers, with varying degrees of success. Castor oil plant, which is highly toxic, also repels them. Both have some effectiveness against moles. Plant garlic, onions, or ornamental alliums to deter woodchucks. Plant garden rue to discourage cats.

7

CHEAP SKILLS

What sets the best gardeners apart from the average ones? Believe it or not, the answer is not money. A hefty budget certainly helps cover up mistakes, such as being able to afford to throw out a dead plant and put in a new one. But what really separates the great gardeners from averages ones are knowledge and skill. Knowledge comes from reading, other gardeners, and experience. Don't be afraid to ask questions. Skill is the action of knowledge. Put what you learn into practice, and watch it pay off.

Read and Record

Good gardeners can learn important new skills from reading. You don't need to squander a fortune on gardening books or magazines. That's why libraries exist. Of course, some books are valuable references you may want to keep close at hand. Don't be too shy to ask for the books you really want on gift-giving occasions. Take notes from interesting magazine articles and organize them into a scrapbook. Above all else, keep reading. Something new is always sprouting in the gardening world.

Another helpful, non-gardening skill that really pays off is record keeping. Keep a comparative record of annual first and last frost dates.

Record the date you plant, the variety, how much (including the number of seeds or square footage) you plant, days to *actual* harvest, amount of harvest, and any other pertinent information. Remember the importance of crop rotation. Draw a diagram and write down what crops you planted where.

By comparing this information annually, you will eventually fine-tune your gardening practices to perfectly suit your situation. Well-kept records will also show you exactly where you spend your gardening dollars. Set a goal each year to cut costs in at least one of your gardening expense areas.

You Can't Afford Not to Mulch

Mulching saves money on irrigation, weed killers, and depending on the mulch used, fertilizer. If you don't already use this cost-cutting technique in your garden, now is the time to begin. It boosts harvests, giving you more for your money.

What Mulching Will Do for You

Mulch is a layer of organic materials, such as straw, or inorganic items, such as landscape fabric, placed on the soil around plants. Either type creates a barrier above the soil. Mulch smothers out weeds and prevents weed seeds from sprouting or landing in your garden from the wind. It holds moisture, and protects plant roots by insulating against extreme temperature fluctuations. It can even help feed plants.

Mulching Materials

Organic mulches work well in flower and vegetable gardens. They have the advantage of breaking down over time to supply nutrients and humus to the soil. For best results, organic mulches should be fairly coarse to prevent them from packing down and matting together. Compacted mulches prevent water from passing through. The mulch must be deep enough so weeds can't poke through, making it useless.

Use inorganic mulches in gardens or landscaping. Inorganic mulches last longer than organic mulches. One negative aspect is they create a barrier preventing organic matter from being added to the soil beneath. Cover sheets of fabric mulches with a layer of soil or organic mulch to protect them from sun damage.

MONEY-SAVING MULCHES

MULCH	DEPTH	DESCRIPTION	WHERE TO FIND IT CHEAP
Alfalfa	6"	Excellent mulch. Contains the plant growth hormone triacontanol, high in nitrogen, and trace minerals.	Buy feeder quality, old or partially rotted hay. (It's less attractive to animals and farmers and fine for mulch.)
Shredded Bark	3"–4"	Attractive.	Landscape supply companies.
Compost	4"	Excellent; feeds soil.	Your compost pile.
Grass Clippings	4"–6"	Let dry first so they don't clump and mat. Be sure they are herbicide-free.	Rake from your own or neighbors' lawns.
Gravel	2"–4"	Decorative, but lets weeds through. Best if applied over another type of mulch. Keep out of the vegetable garden.	Landscape suppliers.
Landscape Fabric	Single layer	Best around shrubs, but it's expensive.	Landscape companies.
Shredded Leaves	4"–6"	Good mulch.	Collect your neighbors'. (You may even get paid to take them!)
Newspaper	Several layers	So, so mulch. Cover with dirt. Don't use colored print.	Collect from neighbors, or local dump or recycling center.
Plastic	Single layer	Warms soil. Weigh down with rocks or other covering.	Salvage from packaging. Use big sheets or overlap smaller pieces.
Salt Hay	4"–6"	Good mulch. Avoid grass hay — it's loaded with seeds.	Gather from fields or purchase at feed stores.
Seaweed	4"–6"	Good mulch.	Collect in coastal areas.
Straw	6"–8"	Good mulch.	If possible buy from the farmer's field (about $1/50-pound bale).
Wood chips, shavings, or sawdust	3"–4"	OK, but add a cup of 21–0–0 or ½ cup 43–0–0 per 100' to counter nitrogen depletion.	Sawmills; landscape supply companies.

Use Mulch to Manipulate Soil Temperature

Once in place, mulch affects soil temperature, and therefore can effectively be used to manipulate growing conditions. For most crops it is best to mulch in the spring after the soil is warm, because it helps to hold in soil warmth. Use plastic mulch to magnify the sun's heat and warm the soil beneath. Heat-loving crops, such as melons and peppers, really benefit from toasty feet. Although black plastic heats up more than clear, the clear plastic transmits more heat through to the soil. You also can mulch cool-season crops, such as spinach or broccoli, earlier in the growing season to keep the soil cool near their roots.

Although a properly applied mulch allows for the free passage of water, do not mulch parched soil. Saturate the soil before mulching to hold moisture in.

Low-Cost Raised Beds

Some gardeners have a long, hard row to hoe, while others work in raised beds. Gardening in raised beds has several economic advantages over rows in a flat plot. The growing beds are separate from pathways, so you can apply fertilizers and soil amendments only where needed, which eliminates waste. Soil in raised beds does not compact and is easy to work by hand, eliminating rototiller expense. Crops can be grown close together, which maximizes the harvest return for the space used. Raised beds create better drainage and the increased surface area causes the soil to warm quickly in the spring, increasing the production of flowers and vegetables alike.

Raise Your Beds, Not Your Expenses

The practice saves money, but often the set-up is so expensive that the payoff takes years to realize. To save money, construct beds from landscape timbers, hewn logs, cement blocks, brick, stone, or any suitable material on hand. As with containers, avoid using treated or painted lumber. The least expensive beds, however, are freestanding.

To create the cheapest, yet just as efficient and good-looking, raised beds, all you need is a shovel. If the plot has not already been cultivated, rent a rototiller first to break up the ground and till in amendments. To design your raised beds over the garden area, run twine between stakes to designate the beds and path-

MONEY-SAVING TIP
Maximize your harvest in a limited space, by planting in raised beds.

ways. You can make the beds any shape or length. Leave about 18 inches between beds to allow enough room for you to work. Make the beds narrow enough to plant or weed from either side without ever having to step into the prepared soil. This prevents plant-stunting soil compaction inevitable in row gardens.

Once the layout is complete, shovel the topsoil from the pathways, along with liberal amounts of compost or other organic soil amendments, into the beds. This puts the best soil where it will do the most good, while elevating the soil level in the beds. With a rake, flatten the topsoil in the beds.

For maximum efficiency, maintain the beds in the same spot every year. Mulch or manure in the fall to shield the surface from windborne weed seeds and insects. Check the beds early in the spring. Due to improved drainage and warmth, they will be ready to plant sooner than you may expect. Spade, rake, and start planting.

Train to Gain

Another cheap skill that can really improve a garden's output is trellising. This practice utilizes vertical space by training otherwise ground-hogging crops to climb a support. Since trellised plants cover less ground space, they use water more efficiently, are less work to weed, receive more sunlight, have better disease-preventing air circulation, and are easier to manage for pest control. All of this adds up to increased yields with less input and expense.

Trellising Made Easy — and Cheap

All you need to trellis a vining plant is a support that may or may not require a framework. Some vines will scramble up the support unaided, while others need to be periodically positioned and tied into place.

As with raised beds, the set-up can be more expensive than the crop is worth. But you don't need to overspend on trellises. Inexpensive trellises work as well as expensive ones — and even the cheapest trellis looks wonderful covered in healthy green or flowering vines. Construct a cheap trellis for pole beans by stringing a line between two support posts and tying strands to it. Once the bean seedlings reach the ends of the strands they *grab on* and climb up, quickly hiding the string. Weave twine between support posts to train other vines. A section of salvaged welded or woven-wire fencing suspended between posts, or dangled from an eave vanishes from view as green growth covers it. Watch climbing vines transform pole or bamboo teepees into green pyramids. If the support is strong, the plants will supply the beauty.

Build your trellises for convenience as well as cost. A favorite of mine is a ladder-style A-frame made of 1-inch by 2-inch lumber and hinged at the top. It will support any vining plant from beans to cantaloupe, lasts for years, and flattens easily for storage.

For the winter, bring this trellis indoors and use it as a clothes-drying rack.

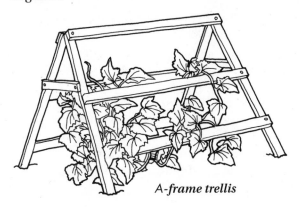

A-frame trellis

SOME PLANTS SUITABLE FOR TRELLISING

Beans
Blackberries
Bougainvillea
Cantaloupe
Clematis
Climbing roses
Cucumber
Grapes
Honeysuckle
Jasmine
Melons
Passion flower
Raspberries
Scarlet runner bean
Sweet potatoes
Tomatoes
Trumpet vine
Wisteria

Easy post frame for pole beans

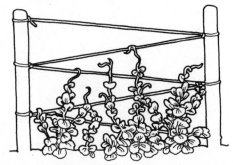

Posts with horizontal twine to train vines

Consider Long-Term Support

For permanent fixtures such as climbing roses the main consideration is an accessible support. Long-lived vines require pruning and other maintenance that annual crops don't need. If trellises are near the house, keep them at least 1 foot from the walls to allow for adequate ventilation, as well as maintenance to the vine and house. Consider that some vining plants, such as wisteria, become very heavy with age and require strong supports. A rambler rose weaving through an old apple tree is a glorious sight, but vines and trees must compete for food, water, and light. Make sure both plants receive what they need.

Prune and Pinch More Than Pennies

Pruning is the brave act of cutting off parts of a plant in the hopes of making it better. It makes plants more vigorous by concentrating growth into the remaining stems. It also makes them healthier by eliminating weak or diseased stems and allowing more light and air to remaining stems and foliage. Pruning controls the shape, flowering, or fruiting of plants. In short, pruning improves plants.

Pruning Pointers

To get started, you need a pair of gloves, a good set of pruning shears, or a sharp knife. For larger branches, you need a pair of loppers, occasionally a saw, and a working knowledge of the particular plant. Some plants flower or fruit on the current year's growth, others on year-old wood, and some on wood of different ages. Knowing which stems are the productive ones is crucial to a good pruning job. Otherwise you may cut off limbs about to flower.

Timing is also important. Prune plants that bloom on the current season's growth in late spring or early winter.

▬ PLANTS TO PRUNE IN LATE SPRING OR EARLY WINTER ▬

CLIMBERS	SHRUBS	PERENNIALS
Trumpet vine	Butterfly bush	Chrysanthemums
Large-flowered	Hardy fuschia	Rudbeckia
clematis	Hibiscus	
Passion flower	Hydrangea	
Plumbago	Western spirea	
Climbing rose		
Grapes		
Honeysuckle		

Early spring also is a good time to remove old or dead wood, and shape species that flower on year-old wood.

PLANTS TO PRUNE IN EARLY SPRING

CLIMBERS	SHRUBS	PERENNIALS
Anemone clematis	Cotoneaster	Delphinium
Bougainvillea	Forsythia	
Hoya	Italian jasmine	
Climbing hydran-	Lacecap and	
gea	mophead hydran-	
Jasmine	gea	
Rambler roses	Lilac	
Wisteria	Mock orange	
	Weigela	

Wait until after the shrubs have flowered, however, to cut them back.

Many blooming shrubs, such as the rampantly growing butterfly bush form thick tangles of spindly growth unless pruned annually. Regular thinning promotes strong, new growth from the base of the plant. It also prevents the loss of bloom quality that accompanies twiggy growth. Not all plants require hours of pruning, however. Many plants, such as the flowering pagoda dogwood, Daphne, camellias, hibiscus, and deciduous Viburnum, prosper with minimal pruning.

Small fruits and fruit trees have special requirements for optimal production, including the following:

→ Cut spent canes of summer-bearing canefruits, such as blackberries and raspberries, to the ground as soon as they finish fruiting.

→ Cut fall-bearing raspberries to the ground in late winter.

→ For blueberries, which produce fruit on two- and three-year-old wood, remove a few branches of the oldest wood each winter to spur the formation of new stems. Severe pruning produces less but larger berries, as well as more new growth.

→ Apples and pears produce fruit from two-year-old and older wood as well as on spurs. Plums yield fruit at the base of young wood and on two-year-old branches. Peaches, nectarines, and apricots bear fruit primarily on one-year-old wood. For untrained trees, winter pruning promotes new growth and creates an open, more productive shape. For those trained to a particular shape, prune in the summer to maintain that training.

Many plants and trees produce more fruit if thinned, such as the following:

→ **Grapes.** Remove smallest flower clusters from grape vines, leaving about 1 foot between remaining bunches. Snip off parts of developing bunches to create that classic grape-cluster shape and to improve the size and quality of the still-forming individual grapes. If the cluster is in the shade, pull off a leaf or two as the grapes begin to ripen to increase the amount of sunlight the grapes receive.

→ **Apples.** Pinch out apple-tree blossoms or wait until after the "June drop," when trees naturally drop imperfect fruit. Thin fruit to an average of 6 inches apart.

→ **Pears.** Thin pears to one or two per cluster, after the natural fruit drop.

→ **Plums.** Thin large-fruited cultivars of plums leaving 3 to 4 inches between fruit. Thin small-fruited varieties leaving 2 to 3 inches between fruit.

→ **Peaches and nectarines.** Early in the season, thin to one fruit from each cluster. Space fruits from 6 to 9 inches apart during the season.

→ **Cherries.** These trees don't require thinning.

Pruning Methods

Here are some basic pruning rules that apply to all plants. To begin, remove dead or diseased wood. Cut below the soil line if possible. You can tell if a stem is dead by scraping the bark with a sharp knife. If the tissue beneath the bark is green, then the branch is alive. If it is yellow, the stem is alive but ailing. If you find brown or grey colors, then the branch is dead. Diseased wood may have cankers, which are dark, depressed spots. Diseased wood also may show blotches, spots, or other obvious signs of illness. Next cut off spindly, overcrowded, or poorly placed stems, flush with the main branch. Finally, you may have to remove some limbs just because there are too many growing for a healthy plant to support.

How many stems to remove depends on the plant and your desired results. For instance, prune cane fruits, such as raspberries, back to no more than seven or eight canes on one plant. More canes lower fruit production. Another example is the hybrid tea rose. If you remove more stems, they produce fewer, but larger flowers.

Once you remove extraneous stems, many plants need the remaining branches shortened. Some plants, such as many varieties of clematis and passion flower, can be cut back to the ground. For some others, remove only the tips to spur new growth.

Every cut you make will have a consequence. If you prune above a bud, it will sprout and grow in the direction it faces. Cut at a slant above and away from the chosen bud, about ⅛ inch to ¼ inch above it. The last bud on the stem becomes the leader or the new end of the stem.

Don't spend money on wound-dressing ointments. A properly made pruning cut will heal itself. There is no clear evidence that dressings reduce wood rots associated with pruning. Proper cuts reduce damage.

These are very general guidelines, compared to the volumes written on precise pruning and training techniques. But if you never do more than mentioned here, you will still improve your investment. For best results, learn about your specific plants.

Practice Pinching

A good pinch now and then is one of the best kept secrets to full-bloomers. Pinching out growing tips early in the season causes the plant to develop lateral buds lower on the plant. These buds fill in to give the plant a full, bushy shape. They also develop more flower buds, and when the plant comes into bloom there are more blossoms.

For perennials, such as rudbeckia and chrysanthemum, wait until the plant is about one-third of its mature size. Pinch back the top 1 or 2 inches of each shoot. Spread this job over a few days, and you will increase the plant's flowering time. The ones you pinch first will bloom first, and the rest will bloom in succession of pinching.

Pinch back annuals, such as petunias, that tend to get leggy if left alone. Snap them off to a joint. This is also a good trick to force a bed of plants into uniform growth. Pinching removes the buds that would have bloomed first, and delays flowering. You may want to leave a few intact for early color, and pinch them after the rest of the flowers are in bloom.

Pinching out growing tips encourages growth of buds below.

Disbudding is a form of pinching that produces outstanding blossoms. You can trick flowers that tend to bloom in bunches — such as dahlias, certain roses, and chrysanthemums — into producing one outstanding bloom where they would have produced several less-dazzling flowers. Choose the largest (usually the center) bud and pinch out all others to the stem. This forces the plant's energy into producing that one perfect bloom.

Finally, deadheading, or removing spent blossoms, is a necessary evil among flowering plants. Pinch or cut out dead flowers before the plant begins to put its energy into producing seeds. This encourages the plant to put out more flowers.

8

LANDSCAPE FOR LESS

What makes some gardens so irresistible? Often it's a cunning focal point or a clever use of plants. Create your own special effects without going into debt.

Accessories on a Shoestring

A cheap garden doesn't have to look plain. On the contrary, the fascinating finds that some frugal gardeners incorporate into their plots often call for a second look. Create a focal point or a functional addition to your garden with nothing more than your imagination and instinct.

Finders Cheapers

One important consideration when looking for cheap accessories is personal taste. Unless you are trying to make a point, nothing should stand out in your garden more than your plants. For instance, plant supports should not show after the plants have grown to their mature size. On the other hand, some finds, such as a weathered old wooden stepladder, blend into the garden scheme wonderfully as obvious plant supports.

Finally, the biggest rule of garden recycling is to learn to think like a plant, sort of. Plants don't care how their needs are met, as long as they are met. If the appearance of plastic milk jugs leaking into your tomato

Rules For Recycling

As a thrifty gardener, always look for free or cheap things to use in your garden. One man's trash is another man's trellis. Follow these rules for recycling:

→ **Make sure** any material you find to use in a vegetable garden is free of toxins.

→ **Don't** use rainbarrels that once contained any form of poison, including petroleum products.

→ **Don't** use railroad ties or landscape timbers that have been treated with a lead-based paint, or a wood preservative, other than copper napthanate. The chemicals will leach into the soil.

→ **Don't** use grass clippings from a lawn treated with a weed and feed type product. (Let at least 2 or 3 mowings go by before you use clippings from a treated lawn.)

→ **Don't** use old tires for growing food — chemical residues in the tire may leach into the crops.

plants is embarrassing, simply bury the jugs next to the transplants and save money proudly!

I don't suggest you have a junk yard theme, but many fabulous finds await you in items other people have thrown away. You can turn an old piece of farm machinery, a beached rowboat or an old gate into a garden centerpiece. All it takes is imagination.

Old wagon wheels are popular garden props. Recreate the look by sectioning a round herb garden with spokes made of dowel or evenly sized, trimmed branches. Use an old ladder to create a neatly sectioned herb or flower bed. Gnarled driftwood, large stones, and other natural items make wonderful centerpieces.

Garden Benches

For those with the tools, time, and skill, building an attractive garden bench makes a fine project. Use redwood for a weather-resistant bench, and coat with a wood preservative.

If you have some planks — preferably sanded and coated with varnish for a smooth, long-lasting sitting surface — and two sections of post, you have the materials for a bench. Sink the posts into the ground so the tops reach a comfortable height for sitting, around 2 feet high.

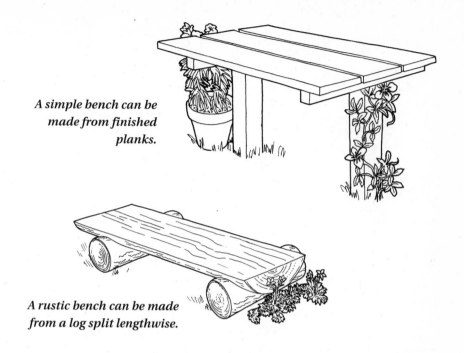

A simple bench can be made from finished planks.

A rustic bench can be made from a log split lengthwise.

Fasten a piece of board with 2-inch or larger wood screws to each post, and attach planks to these boards lengthwise. The dimensions depend on the materials available and your needs. This is a very plain, rustic bench. But a few potted plants, clinging vines, or flowering plants will transform it into a work of beauty.

Instead of a bench, try adding a garden swing. Suspend a section of thick plank with rope from a sturdy tree branch for an old-fashioned tree swing.

My favorite garden bench looked like it was made by Fred Flintstone. It was built from a 5-foot long section of log split lengthwise, and two 2-foot lengths of the same tree. The 2-foot sections were carved to fit snugly against the rounded side of the log, and it was *solid.*

If you opt to splurge on a store-bought bench, go with wrought iron. It will probably outlast the garden. Hardwood benches may cost several times as much and may not last nearly as long.

You can substitute many items for a traditional garden bench. Outcast wicker furniture fits well into a garden theme. Use an air compressor or stiff brush to remove flaking old paint, repaint, and finish with a coat of clear varnish or other sealant. Unsplit firewood rounds serve as unobtrusive gardener perches. For a softer settee, settle yourself on a bale of hay or straw, but toss a cover over it if you are wearing shorts!

You can make an inexpensive birdbath from an old aluminum garbage can lid.

The lid can be hung from a sling padded with moss.

Birdbath Basics

Birds add so much to the garden and ask very little in return. One surefire way to draw their attention is to provide them with a source of water, a necessity for other beneficial organisms as well.

An old aluminum garbage can lid, turned over, holds water wonderfully. Set it on the ground, a few feet from any plants that may provide cat-cover. Scatter a little gravel on the bottom of the lid for footing and fill with water. Arrange a few stones or overflowing plants around the rim to disguise the lid's true identity. If you prefer an elevated birdbath, hang the lid in a rope sling, pad the sling with moss, and nestle the lid into it for a decorative effect.

You can build a stonelike birdbath by mixing equal parts portland concrete, milled peat moss, and mason sand with just enough water to make it cling together; this mixture is called hypertufa. Pour the mixture into a plastic-lined mold, such as an old birdbath or a garbage can lid, about 1½ inches thick against the bottom and edges. Let dry a day or two then remove the plastic, and stress the exposed edges for a hewn stone look. Chip with a chisel, hack with a hatchet, and scrub with a wire brush for the realistic look of handcarved stone. Set aside in a warm, dry spot to cure for four to six weeks, then finish curing for another few weeks in the weather to neutralize the cement. Frequent watering helps leach out chemicals. Rinse with vinegar to neutralize alkalinity.

MONEY-SAVING TIP
Make your own stonelike birdbath from hypertufa mixture.

Consider a Pond

Something about the reflective serenity of a garden pond draws visitors to pause and ponder. Garden natives rely on it for moisture and a cool refuge. Its presence fosters beneficial insects, birds, and animals. And a whole new class of plant possibilities opens up to the gardener.

A simple pond is low-maintenance. Fancier versions with pumps and lights require more attention, and of course are most expensive. Simplicity is beautiful and cheap.

There are two types of do-it-yourself installation kits available. One type consists of a pre-molded rigid liner, and you must dig a hole to suit the container. The other type uses a flexible plastic sheet liner, which offers the creative freedom of fitting the liner to the hole. Either one makes a lovely garden pond.

To prepare the pond, first mark the outline with a rope or garden hose, then score around the outline with a shovel. Dig until you reach the required depth. Most water-garden plants need at least 6 inches of water, and pond fish, such as goldfish or koi, require a deep end of at least 24 inches as a place to hibernate. If you plan to stock fish in the pond, use a fish-grade liner. Span the hole with a board, and rest a level on top. Make any adjustments necessary to keep the pond level. Shovel in a 3-inch cushion of damp sand, and settle the liner in place.

Flexible liners are less bulky, as well as less expensive. You can create underwater shelves, 9 to 12 inches wide and 9 to 12 inches below the surface, to simulate realistic conditions for pond plants and fish. Also, flexible liners allow you to angle the bottom deeper at one end which causes debris to settle in one spot.

You can substitute other materials for either type of pond for added savings. Use thick black plastic in place of the flexible liner (not recommended with fish), or sink a kid's pool as you would a rigid-liner. Since landscape plants, arranged stones, water plants, and dirt settling to the bottom obscure the pond liner from view, no one will ever know the difference. Large-sized kid's pools go on sale at the end of the summer for a fraction of their original cost.

Double-Duty Dollars

A savvy use of your favorite plants goes a long way toward creating your dream garden, and I don't merely mean having a well-arranged layout, although that is always pleasing. I mean making your plants and your invested dollars pull double duty.

Make a Year-Round Investment

The garden has more to offer than just pretty spring blooms. Consider including a few plants that offer a point of interest beyond the first act — go for the curtain call!

Many plants put on a splendid show in the fall. Let fiery-colored leaves and bright berries decorate your autumn surroundings. The red leaves of Spirea japonica, purples of flowering plums, yellows of the Maidenhair tree and Japanese maples all play the same role as flowers in the summer garden. Berries, in white (snowberry), red (cotoneaster, holly), orange (Mountain ash), and dusky purple (Oregon grape) contribute their own thousand points of light.

Plants providing winter interest give your garden morale a boost when you least expect it, but need it most. Gardeners value many types of roses, including Rugosas, antique 'Old Garden' varieties, and the cultivar `Geranium' for the bright orange to red hips they produce. Not only are they attractive, but they provide welcome winter food for birds. The ptericantha rose has enormous, bright red, 1-inch-wide thorns that become obvious after the foliage drops. Evergreen shrubs, such as Oregon grape, hollies, Junipers and Euonymus, retain their good looks throughout the winter. Try redtwig or yellowtwig dogwood, white-stemmed *Rubus biflorus,* or the twisted branches of the European Filbert 'Contorta' for colorful winter appeal. Use climbers, such as winter-blooming jasmine or evergreen ivies, to accentuate the winter garden.

Hedge on Fences

Let's say you want a line of demarcation to mark your territory. A lesser gardener might think of a fence. But let the creative force in you take over, and you may find a better, probably cheaper, alternative.

Hedges are popular on property lines for many reasons. They look very nice when kept up, and they keep most people on their own side. A negative aspect is the amount of upkeep. The time and expense of trimming and maintaining a hedge is not a real selling point. But what if that hedge required very little upkeep, and offered more than just a boundary line?

Whoever said hedges have to be of boxwood or privet, especially when there are other plants with so much more to offer? Consider some of the following plants for hedges:

→ **Blueberry.** Produces lovely white flowers in spring, luscious berries in summer, and attractive red foliage in fall.

→ **Fruit trees.** Grow apple, pear, peach, plum, or cherry trees in a two-dimensional shape on a trellis. Train the arms, or cordons, of the trees into interlocking patterns to create a living fence.

→ **Grapes.** Fast-growing vines quickly cover a trellis to form a wall of green, attractive leaves, and sumptuous grapes. Plant so the south side is on your side of the property line; this is where the most fruit forms.

→ **Hawthorne.** Provides fragrant flowers, fruit, and fall foliage, as well as enough thorns to keep out any neighbors.

→ **Holly.** Stays attractive year round, forms an impenetrable wall, and even provides Christmas decorations.

→ **Rugosa or shrub roses.** Perfume the air and supply armloads of romantic bouquets and hips for jelly.

Sometimes a fence is a necessity. If you want to contain pets or children, it's a must. They don't have to be ugly, however. Let climbing plants flow over them in a cascade of color and fragrance. Transform a lowly chain-link fence with blossom-bursting annual vines of trailing nasturtium, sweet pea, or morning glories. Put the fence to work supporting a crop of pole beans or garden peas. Perennial vines, such as clematis, climbing rose, trumpet vines, and scores of others, turn a fence into a yearly delight. For a solid wood fence, you can resort to ivies or tack up a few horizontal wires to support other climbers. If you happen to be on the south side of the fence, take advantage of this warmth-creating microclimate. Paint it white and use the space to grow cold tender plants or fabulous fruit.

MONEY-SAVING TIP
Create a rustic garden fence from discarded wooden pallets.

Materials for fencing can be very expensive, but a cheap alternative is waiting for you. Warehouses throw away damaged wooden pallets every day. Collect matching pallets, erect around the garden, and paint if desired. If done well, the humble beginnings of such a garden fence only adds to its rustic charm. Or, you can plant a few vines to disguise it.

A fence camouflaged by a hedge or plant provides more than just privacy. Dense vegetation will buffer sound, and will make your garden a quieter place. Use plants to block an unattractive view, hide the compost pile, or create a gardener's refuge.

9

LONGER LIFE FOR YOUR PLANT DOLLARS

Unless you garden in the tropics, you probably have wished there was just a little more to the growing season. After all, you can only stomach so many green tomatoes. You *can* lengthen the growing season in your garden, using inexpensive season extenders. You can also extend and protect the life of tender landscape plants.

Hot Caps Mean Cold Cash

Hot caps are flimsy, little wax-paper plant covers sold in garden stores. When placed over transplants, they protect from light frost. They are inexpensive and perform the job. But there are cheaper substitutes.

Fight Frost For Free

When making hot caps, or cloches (the generic name for frost-protective plant coverings) use material that will allow sunlight through. Young plants need light to grow, and the covering magnifies the warm air surrounding the transplants. On the morning after a frost, a temperature difference of just a few degrees often makes the difference between a thriving plant and a dead one. Leave the coverings on the plant after the danger of frost has passed, to encourage more vigorous plant growth in the warm, moist microclimate. Remove them as the plants outgrow them, or as the days get warmer.

An improvement over store-bought hot caps are clear plastic bottles. Two-liter soda bottles work well for individual plant protectors. Soak to remove the labels that would otherwise block sunlight, then cut the bottom out of each bottle. Save the cap. With the bottoms removed,

Homemade hot caps from two-liter soda bottles.

stack the bottles for storage. At planting time, position a bottle over each tender transplant, and push the cut end down into the soil to anchor it.

I like these better than their commercial cousins for two reasons. One reason is they are free. You can also unscrew the cap to vent the covering on sunny days. This is important, because heat can build up inside the covering and scorch young plants.

Opaque plastic, 1-gallon bottles, such as those sold containing distilled water or milk, work as well or better than the two-liter size. Their biggest advantage is size. Plants don't outgrow the 1-gallon size as quickly. They also come with a built-in anchor support. Cut the top out of the handle, push a thin stake or piece of bamboo through, and anchor in the soil.

Wire tomato cages also make good plant protectors. Position them over the plant and cover with one or two clear plastic bags. These will accommodate a fairly large plant. Remember to ventilate the cover on sunny, not necessarily hot, days. Wait until the dew dries, and pull off the plastic. Replace the cover in late afternoon so that it can reheat before nightfall.

One store-bought plant protector that is worth the ticket-price and tough to duplicate is the Wall-o'Water. Made of clear plastic compartments, the plant protector holds water, which acts as a solar storage medium. It converts light into warmth by day, stores it, and releases it at night. If properly cared for, the item will last for years.

Recycled Row Covers

Collect clear scrap plastic to make covers large enough for rows or beds. Dry-cleaning bags are thin but usable; use at least two layers. Look for large, heavy-duty plastic bags used by retail stores to cover items such as furniture, mattresses, bedding, and some appliances. They are a great find. Contact retailers, and ask for the bags removed from display models.

Construct a support from salvaged items to hold plastic row or bed covers over plants. Bend PVC pipe, bamboo, or sections of wire mesh over rows or beds, and push the ends into the soil to anchor them. Whatever material you use, make sure it is strong enough to withstand the prevailing winds when covered with plastic.

Use row covers in the spring to protect seedlings, and in the fall to extend the productive life of crops. If used in the spring, remove the plastic covers as the season warms, and leave the frame in place for later use.

Cover crops in the fall to extend their production by weeks. It's the first frost that catches many gardeners off guard, and effectively ends the growing season, even though weeks of warm, sunny days may follow. Prepare your garden early. Call your local weather service to find out if your area is expecting an early frost. Also, watch the evening news to track developing weather patterns.

A plastic covering provides warmth and humidity, but *any* covering over frost-sensitive plants at night can save their lives during a light freeze. Gather old sheets, blankets, bags, curtains, buckets, and mixing bowls, and cover plants before dark.

World's Cheapest Greenhouse

The one function of a greenhouse is to start plants under controlled conditions for early growth. I've always wanted one, but I found a much cheaper alternative.

A cold frame is similar to a greenhouse, only smaller around and much shorter in height. The smaller size of the cold frame makes it much easier to keep warm inside, because there is less space to heat. You can sow seeds directly into prepared soil in the cold frame, or sow in containers for later transplanting.

A cold frame is kept warm by a piece of glass or heavy, clear plastic lid, placed at a 45-degree, south-facing angle. This angle will collect and magnify the rays of the low spring or late fall sun. Place a few rocks or a couple of black-painted water containers inside the cold frame to act as solar collectors. They will store heat, and release it during the night. Make sure the sides of the cold frame are thick enough to insulate from frosty night air. They don't need to conduct light, however.

Build Your Own Cold Frame

Even if you had to go out and purchase materials to build a cold frame, the materials would cost much less than even a tiny greenhouse. Of course, I have other ideas.

There are dozens of plans for cold frames in magazines and books, and some of them get pretty sophisticated, which is great for convenience. But functional can be frugal. First you need a lid. The size of the lid determines the size of the cold frame. Scour classified ads, condemned houses, and garage sales to find an old windowpane or glass-door panel. A scrap lumber frame with heavy, clear plastic stapled to both sides will work, except during severe frost.

For the frame, scrap lumber is a possibility. Old landscape timbers are great, because they are thick enough to insulate well, or you can use plywood or another thin building material and insulate it by mounding at least 4 inches of soil against the exterior sides. Remember to avoid

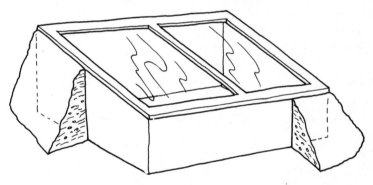

A cold frame made from an old window and scrap lumber.

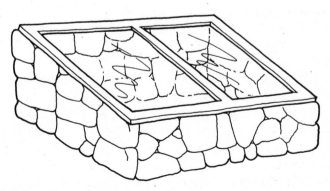

An alternative cold frame structure made with rocks.

A cold frame made from baled straw.

pressure-treated lumber, however. Another alternative is to build a frame from rock or salvaged brick to fit the dimensions of the lid. Rock and brick are cheap, attractive, and very efficient at storing solar energy. Another inexpensive insulating material is straw. It may have failed the first little pig, but baled straw or hay insulates very well. Stack two bales at the north end of the cold frame and also on the sides. Stack one straw bale at the south end. Place the lid so it touches the side bales, for as few air leaks as possible.

Use the cold frame for transplants or winter crops. Place a thermometer inside to monitor when night temperatures in the cold frame are above freezing, or set a glass of distilled water in the frame — when no ice forms in the glass overnight, set out your first transplants. Because seedlings germinate best in warmer temperatures, start them indoors. Transfer seedlings to the cold frame after they develop a few sets of leaves. Direct-seed salad greens, carrots, radishes, and other cool-season crops in the cold frame for fresh, winter vegetables.

Prepare for Winter

A major tragedy for plant lovers is waiting all winter only to find withered, brown remnants where you expected sprouting buds in the spring. One way to avoid this is to plant only cold-hardy varieties as discussed in Chapter 4 (pages 62–73). But for those gardeners who can't resist a tender shrub or perennial, you must tuck them in for the winter.

A Cozy Cover-Up

From low-lying, rock-garden alpines to climbing roses, many perennial plants are at risk when winter arrives. Snow cover helps insulate plants from the dangers of freezing and thawing, but snow is not always reliable.

Begin to toughen perennials and shrubs for winter in late fall. Actually, this is a step nature does for you, just don't interfere. Stop dead-heading — going to seed is a signal plants perceive as a winter warning. Also, cut back on water. This will physically toughen the plant by evacuating as much water as possible from tissues. These signals, combined with decreasing light and falling temperatures cause the plant to become dormant. Plants that are dormant prior to a hard freeze have the best chance of survival.

MONEY-SAVING TIP
Provide winter protection for tender shrubs and roses by creating a 1-foot-deep mound of soil around the base.

The good news is the cheapest way to protect plants is also one of the best. For tender shrubs and roses, the best protection is a one-foot-deep mound of soil at the base of the plant. For grafted plants, including many roses, the extra dirt will protect the vulnerable union where the cultivar attaches to the rootstock. The extra soil also protects the roots, which are the life center of the plant. Add further protection by covering outdoor plants with straw, pine needles, crumpled newspaper, or another bulky material. Wrap the plant and protective materials inside a tarp, sheet of plastic, old feed sack, or old blanket. Secure this insulation with twine or tape. Any perennials or biennials that are not reliably hardy in your area will benefit from a similar cover-up. Some plants get a bad rap for requiring this special treatment, but if you have already made an investment, you should protect it.

You can protect long canes of tender climbing roses by wrapping with insulation. But if you protect the roots, and in most cases the graft, then the plant will survive.

Before the first frost, dig up tender perennials, such as pelargoniums, begonias, and impatiens, and move them inside for the winter if you want to save them. To prepare them for winter storage, shake off as much dirt as possible and trim back the roots and stems. Pot the plants individually, or put them all together in one large container. Keep tender perennials in a cool, but frost-free place, with plenty of light. Water only when the potting mix dries out.

There are a few plants, such as snapdragons, that come back the second season like a bad rerun. They just don't look as good after their first year. Don't bother trying to save them.

10

REAP BOUNTIFUL HARVESTS

After preparing soil, maintaining tools, watering, weeding, feeding, and pampering your plants, don't you think you deserve a rest? Not yet. It's time to harvest the fruits of your labor.

Nothing Beats Free, Fresh Food

Finally, the payoff has arrived. With high-priced fruits and vegetables in the supermarkets and your homegrown food ripe in the garden, it's hard not to hear a little cash register ringing in your head. Unfortunately, this is where many hard-working, cost-conscience gardeners fail. Either they don't bring in the entire harvest, or they don't pick food at its peak ripeness.

It's easy to get excited about the first greens of spring. Most of us even manage to bring in, shell, and prepare early peas, which is no small feat. But by the time warm-season crops ripen, some gardeners begin to lose their enthusiasm. Maybe it's the food's fault for ripening just when you're about to go on vacation or sneak away for a day at the lake. But it's the gardener who pays the price.

Spare yourself the guilt and expense of a wasted harvest by planning realistically when planting. Not every seed you plant will produce actual food, but most of them should. Based on actual grocery-store purchases of fruits and vegetables, or past garden production, try to project how much fresh food your family will use. Then, considering the time it takes to preserve the harvest and your storage capacity, determine how much of your harvest you will be able to put up. Once you plant, consider yourself committed.

Pick at the Peak

Plants only produce fruit and vegetables for one reason — to perpetuate their species. Fruit for its own sake is not on the plant's agenda. The plant has performed its duty only when the fruit has produced seeds. At this point, however, most fruit and vegetables are no longer suitable for consumption. In other words, the harvest is not going to wait for you. It will reach its tender, tasty peak, and then continue to grow towards its destiny. It's up to you to harvest at the right time.

MONEY-SAVING TIP
Plan ahead so you grow just the amount of produce you're able to consume, preserve, and store, to avoid wasting time and resources.

Even poorly timed harvests will probably save you money over food bought from the grocery store. But why settle for less than gourmet quality?

The following table lists common fruits and vegetables, and gives tips on how to tell when they are perfect to harvest. It also tells how to harvest them. Remember, even if part of the fruit is not perfect, perhaps due to physical or insect damage, you can probably still salvage most of it.

SECRETS OF THE PERFECT HARVEST

Apples.   Ripe when background color turns yellow, stem pulls free of the spur just as it is bent upward, seeds have turned brown and it *tastes* ripe. Apples picked unripe stay spongy. To harvest grasp fruit and gently lift up. Be careful not to damage the fruiting spur so it may continue to produce next year. For fruit high on the tree, use a long-handled fruit picker to cradle the apple, then lift.

Apricots.   Ripe when deeply colored, slightly soft and fruit comes free of the stem with a gentle twist. To harvest tip fruit sideways and twist gently. Be very careful not to bruise.

Asparagus.   Ripe when spears are 5 to 8 inches tall. To harvest cut below ground-level with a sharp knife. Harvest for 8 to 10 weeks.

Green or Snap Beans. Ripe when pods are full-sized, but before seeds begin to swell. To harvest grasp bean in one hand and vine in the other, and quickly, but gently snap. Don't twist or pull. Harvesting encourages further production.

Pick vegetables at their peak to get the most from your harvest.

Lima Beans. Ripe when pods begin to swell. Harvest the same as green or snap beans.

Shell Beans. Ripe when pods are nearly dry on the vine. To harvest snap free of vine.

Beets. Ripe when green tops appear, and roots are about 2 inches across. To harvest pick at base of plant. Grasp base of tops and pull firmly.

Blackberries. Ripe when glossy berries just begin to lose their shine, or they drop at a touch. To harvest pick early in the morning into a shallow berry bucket or container.

Blueberries. Ripe when a few days have passed *after* berries have turned blue. Most ripen over a 2- to 5-week period. To harvest roll berries between the fingers, picking only the ripe ones. Attach a berry-bucket to a belt loop to free hands.

Broccoli. Ripe when the main head has formed into tight, green buds. Don't wait until they begin to open. Same for side shoots, which will form after the main head is cut. To harvest cut out the main head leaving enough stalk to produce side shoots.

Brussels Sprouts. Ripe when buds are less than 1 inch in diameter. To harvest cut buds from the stalk, then remove the leaf from below each. Harvest from bottom of the stalk up. Cut the top of the plant off in August to promote bud ripening. Frost improves the flavor, so if possible wait until after the first couple of frosts to harvest.

Cabbage. Ripe when heads are large and still firm. If left in the garden too long it becomes tough and fibrous, and the head splits. Once the head has developed to maturity prevent furtheraging by cutting through the taproot with a shovel. To harvest cut at base of plant. Or for cabbages that are to be stored, pull them up roots and all.

Cantaloupe. Ripe when creamy colored with pronounced netting; vine begins to crack at base of fruit and slips off easily. To harvest use only a gentle tug. Any that must be pulled are not yet ripe.

Carrots. Ripe when fully colored. Most are best if harvested before 1½ inches across as they get woody with age. To harvest grasp tops near base of plant and pull gently upwards.

Cauliflower. Ripe when white heads are 6 to 10 inches across, and before the curds begin to separate. To harvest cut head out at base of plant or pull up, roots and all.

Celery. Ripe when stalks form. To harvest cut at base or dig up entire plant. Harvest self-blanching types before frost.

Cherries. Ripe when fully colored for the variety, and when they pass the taste test. Birds flocking to the tree mean its time to pick quickly! Harvest individually or in bunches. Use a container strapped to a belt loop to free your hands.

Corn. Ripe when pricked kernels exude a milky rather than clear liquid. Usually about 18 days after silks have appeared. They will be dry and brown by this time. If the liquid is gummy, then the corn is past its prime but may still be okay for canning. To harvest grasp ear near stalk and pull down quickly and firmly.

Cucumbers. Ripe when slightly immature, about 2 to 6 inches long for picklers and 6 to 10 inches for slicers. Lemon cukes will be 3 to 4 inches round and light yellow. To harvest cut or pinch, leaving at least 1 inch of the vine on the fruit. This slows deterioration due to water loss.

Eggplant. Ripe when stem is woody but before the skin loses its gloss, about 3 to 5 inches long for most types. To harvest cut, leaving a bit of stem. Remove any flowers or small fruit late in the season, to promote ripening of remaining fruit.

Garlic. Ripe when plant top has dried out. To harvest dig bulbs and remove or braid stems.

Grapes. Ripe when they taste like it. Color is not a sure indicator. To harvest gently snap or snip clusters from the vine.

Herbs. Ripe when leaves have reached full size for the species. To harvest pick individual leaves or snap stems off at ground and strip leaves. Leafy herbs are best if you harvest them in the morning.

Jerusalem Artichoke.   Ripe when touched by first frost. To harvest dig tubers and cut away stems.

Kale.   Ripe when leaves are tender. To harvest pick youngest leaves from center of plant or cut entire plant at the base.

Kiwi.   Ripe when fruit just begins to soften to the touch. To harvest clip hardy kiwi with a bit of vine, fuzzy types without. Be very careful not to bruise.

Lettuce and Greens.   Ripe when at least 2 inches long until plant begins to bolt (go to seed). To harvest pick individual leaves as needed or cut plant at base. Wait until head lettuce fills out and feels firm.

Okra.   Ripe when pods are 2 to 4 inches long and snap off easily. To harvest grasp each pod and snap. Watch out for the spines.

Onions.   Ripe when green stems sprout for green onions or after the plant falls over and dries for bulbs. To harvest dig carefully, don't bruise. Let cure in the sun for a few days. Braid tops or clip off.

Peas.   Ripe when pods are filled out, but are still smooth. Once they get lumpy or develop a whitish cast they will be hard and bitter. Snow peas are ready as soon as pods are about 3 inches long. To harvest grasp pod in one hand and vine in other, and snap free. Be careful not to damage the vine and it will keep producing as long as you keep picking, or until hot weather halts production.

Peaches and Nectarines.   Ripe when fully colored and just soft. If picked before maturity, they will continue to ripen somewhat off the tree. To harvest grasp and pull. Be very careful not to bruise, especially with nectarines.

Pears.   Ripe when full size and have a hint of mature color. Fruit comes free when gently tipped. Don't allow pears to ripen fully on the tree, because they get mushy. Leave at room temperature for a few days to develop the best flavor and texture. To harvest tip up, and fruit ready to pick separates easily.

Peppers.   Ripe when full sized. May be picked green or allowed to color depending on the variety. To harvest snap from stem. Get all before frost.

Plums.   Ripe when fully colored for the variety (which varies greatly) and the flesh has softened slightly. To harvest grasp and snap free.

Taste one or two to make sure they are ready because they won't ripen off the tree.

Potatoes. Ripe when plants flower for new potatoes, and after the vines are yellow and withered for full-size spuds. To harvest carefully dig with a spade or garden fork. Try not to nick any potatoes. Do not let spuds sit in sunlight, because they get green and bitter.

Rhubarb. Ripe when stalks are about ½ inch across and blushing. To harvest cut stalks at ground-level, remove leaves. Continue for four weeks, then let plant rest until next season.

Rutabagas, Parsnips, and Turnips. Ripe when touched by a few light frosts. To harvest dig carefully. Cut off tops, to within about 1 inch of root.

Spinach. Ripe when leaves are big enough to eat. To harvest pull individual leaves or cut plant at base. Spinach is best if you harvest in the morning.

Summer squash. Ripe when moderately sized, well colored, and skin is still soft. To harvest pull free from stem, leaving a bit of vine on each fruit.

Winter Squash and Pumpkins. Ripe when fully colored for the variety and skin has toughened. Most are best after the first light frost. To harvest cut from the vine, leaving about 2 inches of stem on each.

Sweet Potatoes. Ripe when full size. Either immediately after a very light frost or before any frost. To harvest dig *very* carefully to avoid root damage. Start a few feet from vines and work in.

Tomatoes. Ripe when fully colored for the variety. Pick if frost threatens. Those that show color will ripen somewhat off the vines. Those that don't show color may be eaten green. To harvest grasp and snap free.

Watermelons. Ripe when the last tendril of the leaf nearest the fruit dies, the skin gets rough, and the fruit echoes when thumped. To harvest thump-test in the morning. Slip from the vine.

Stocking the Pantry

As you bring in your harvest, let's compare the storage costs. Drying or dehydrating, canning, freezing, and storing food in a root cellar vary in cost, longevity, and quality, depending on the produce. The best results usually come from a combination of methods. For instance, store carrots and potatoes in a root cellar, dehydrate fruit snacks, can fruits or green beans, and freeze broccoli, corn, and peas.

Root-Cellar Storage

This old-time method of food preservation is just as practical now as it ever was in the past. It is the easiest, least expensive, and simplest way to keep certain crops. To successfully store crops for any length of time you have to know a little about their individual storage requirements. Once these details are known, the process is very reliable. If a spud, carrot, or orange has deteriorated in storage, you will know it at first glance. Spoiled foods from root collars are instantly recognizable. If a spud looks bad, smells bad, and even feels bad, then you know it is bad.

The only downside to this type of storage in modern times is the lack of a root cellar facility in new homes. You can use a substitute facility with varying degrees of success with each year and each new crop. Unheated sheds, basements, crawl-spaces, barns, and the undersides of stairwells may all serve as root cellars.

A well-stocked root cellar or pantry is the dirt-cheap gardener's pay-off.

Thrifty and inventive gardeners have created various outdoor, make-shift root cellars. Pits in the ground or built into a bank, either natural or man-made, are among the most common outside versions of root cellars. A good tip is to line a pit or trench with wire hardware cloth to keep out winter-starved rodents. An out-of-work winter cold frame works well. An old refrigerator, salvaged from a dump or repair shop and buried on its back, makes a nifty storage box. For safety, make sure you dismantle any door-locking mechanism. You can also bury discarded styrofoam coolers or use them in storage areas.

You can get most supplies necessary for root-cellar storage, either free or cheap. Use barrels, crates, cardboard boxes, and baskets for fruit and vegetable containers. To pack produce in containers, try using newspaper, wood shavings, sawdust, dried leaves, clean, damp builders' sand, or peat moss. Packing food holds in moisture and slows respiration by limiting the exchange of oxygen. Old pantyhose or netting make useful bags for hanging onions or oranges.

Food preparation for root-cellar storage is minimal. For most vegetables, cut stems back to approximately 1 inch to minimize moisture

═══ FOODS SUITABLE FOR ROOT CELLARING ═══

Apples	Endive	Pears
Dry beans	Grapes	Peppers
Beets	Horseradish**	Potatoes
Cabbage	Kale**	Pumpkins and
Carrots**	Onions	squash
Cauliflower	Oranges and	Rutabagas
Celery**	grapefruit	Tomatoes
Chinese cabbage	Parsnips**	Turnips

**A very few crops will store themselves in the garden. All they need is a mulch to keep them from freezing and thawing. Horseradish, parsnips, and salsify will winter over beautifully if, once frozen, they are kept that way. Keep celery going for months by mounding soil up the sides of the plant in the fall. Keep adding soil as the weather cools, until only the tips of the plants are visible. Mulch endive and kale the same way. Carrots will keep fairly well if covered with a thick (18–24 inch) mulch of straw. And Jerusalem Artichokes stay delicious throughout the winter if treated this way. Just remember that you have to get to garden wintered crops — through snow or whatever.

loss from within the vegetable. Then cure for a few days in the sun or a warm, dry place. This toughens the skin for storage. Gently brush off as much dirt as possible, but do not wash. Store fruits and vegetables at the peak of maturity and in a cool place. Here are the most important points of successful root-cellar storage:

→ Use the late-maturing crops for best results in root-cellar storage. This means you must plan at planting time for crops to mature late in the season. Most unripe crops will not store well. Pears and tomatoes are notable exceptions.

→ Store only recommended foods.

→ Use only food-safe containers, including plastic bags. Garbage bags and other plastics not made for food may contain germicides or hazardous levels of cadmium or other chemicals.

→ Never store fruits near vegetables. Fruits absorb odors and flavors. Fruits' respiration of ethylene gas also may affect the storage quality of vegetables. Never store apples near potatoes.

→ Store cabbage separately; the odor is so strong it will permeate other foods, even your house if stored in the basement. A heavily mulched, outdoor pit works best to store cabbage.

→ Make the storage compartment dark; cover all windows.

→ Try to give the storage area good ventilation, but it is more important to maintain an even, cool temperature.

→ If using an underground pit, remove all exposed rocks from inside the pit, because they conduct frost from outside. Dig a drainage ditch leading away from the storage area. Use plenty of packing material in and around containers. If you disturb the pit, you may have to bring its entire contents indoors. You may want to prepare several small caches as opposed to a large one.

As previously mentioned, different fruits and vegetables have different requirements for optimum storage. Some crops, such as peppers, sweet potatoes, and tomatoes, require warmer conditions than most. Other items, such as onions, dried beans, and peas, need very low humidity. Catering to such individual requirements can be a challenge, depending on your facilities. Remember that heat rises. If you are storing food in a basement or shed, put food requiring warmth on the top shelves, place food with cool temperature requirements near the bottom. For more information on root-cellaring, consult *Root Cellaring*, by Mike and Nancy Bubel (see "Recommended Reading List," page 157).

Dehydrating

The practice of dehydrating has been used to preserve food for centuries before expensive dehydrators were created. Dehydrating is one of the least expensive methods of food preservation available. Even if you splurge on a dehydrator, whether homemade or commercial, it will eventually pay for itself.

Hikers, hunters, and backpackers prefer dried food, because it is lightweight. Homemade dried food always tastes better and is less expensive than the freeze-dried version sold at specialty stores. Storing dried food is inexpensive and space-efficient.

You can dehydrate almost any food. You may not like the taste or texture of some dried food, however. The shelf life of dried food is usually longer than for that of other food-preservation methods. But moisture affects storage; a little moisture invites spoilage.

Prepare foods for drying by first washing off any traces of dirt and then patting very dry. You can dry small, evenly sized produce, such as peas, beans, grapes, or apricots, whole, but cut larger produce, such as apples, carrots, or onions, into uniform slices. This facilitates even dry-

══════ RECOMMENDED FOODS FOR DEHYDRATING ══════

Food	Texture When Dried	Food	Texture When Dried
Apples	Pliable to slightly crisp	Peas	Wrinkled and brittle
		Peaches	Leathery
Apricots	Pliable	Pears	Leathery
Beans		Peppers	Tough
(green)	Hard and brittle	Hot peppers	Crispy
Beets	Brittle (cracks when bent)	Plums	Pliable
		Potatoes	Crisp
Carrots	Hard and brittle	Rhubarb	Tough
Cherries	Leathery	Strawberries	Pliable
Corn	Shrivelled and crunchy	Sunflowers	Hard
		Tomatoes	Crispy
Fruit leather	Leathery		
Garlic	Crisp		
Grapes	Wrinkled and leathery		
Herbs (leaves or flowers)	Papery crisp		
Onions	Papery		
Parsnips	Crisp to brittle		

ing. Thin slices dry faster than thick ones. Slices between ⅛-inch and ⅜-inch thick dry best. Dry fruits and herbs from their raw form. Vegetables store better if you first blanch them in water or over steam. Due to their low acid content, vegetables are prone to spoilage, and you must dry them more completely than fruit. You may wish to treat with sulfur to hasten drying, improve color, retard spoilage, and repel insects. Sulfur is not necessary, however, and many people don't like fruit treated with sulfur.

One of the cheapest ways to dry foods is to sun-dry them, but it only works in dry, sunny areas. Place prepared food on old window screens or cheesecloth frames and cover with a second layer to shield from bugs and birds. Set in the sun by day and bring in before evening or if rain threatens.

A friend of mine in western Oregon, where dry, sunny days are rare, uses a clever substitute for direct sunlight. She sets trays of prepared food in her car, and takes advantage of the heat generated by the windows. Ventilation is not so good, but she usually gets good results. A hot, summer cold frame works the same way.

A variation of sun-drying is air-drying, which you can do indoors. String up apple slices, green beans, or any food through which you can thread a needle or string. Hang strings of food over a furnace vent, near, but not too near, a woodstove, in the attic, or near any other heat source. Space them so there is good air circulation. Drape a piece of cheesecloth over the string to protect from dust and bugs.

Use a low oven, set between 90° and 120°F as a heat source. Of course, electric dehydrators work very well. But don't use the microwave because it ruins fruits and vegetables. Leafy herbs, due to their low water content, dry successfully in the microwave, by placing on a paper towel and drying on high for thirty seconds to one minute at a time. Shuffle the leaves around after each interval and feel for dryness. They should be crispy after three or four attempts.

Drying times vary with the food, size of the pieces, temperature, and humidity of the heat source. Most foods will dry within two or three days in the sun, and within eight to twenty-four hours in a dehydrator. Texture is the best test for doneness (see chart of "Recommended Foods for Dehydrating").

Store dehydrated foods in airtight, pest-proof containers in a dark, cool spot. Check for condensation after the first few days, and return the contents of any moist packages to the dryer.

Use dehydrated foods either dry or reconstituted. Fruit snacks are wonderful dried, and many dried vegetables make tasty, crunchy snacks as well; try adding them to salads, casseroles, or soup.

Pre-soaked vegetables cook quickly. To reconstitute, cover with water and soak for a few hours to overnight. Save the nutritious soaking water, and use it for cooking.

For more detailed information on food drying, along with recipes for using dried foods, see *Making and Using Dried Foods* by Phyllis Hobson. See "Recommended Reading List" page 157.

Home Canning

Home canning brings us into the modern age of food preservation and delivers a host of demons. The pH levels of food, bacteria, processing times, and proper seals are all important concerns in this process. Also, consider the cost of jars, canners, and pressure cookers. Still, canned goods are a reliable staple in any gardener's pantry.

There are different canning methods. A boiling water bath retains temperatures of at least 212°F for the entire processing time. It works fine for canning high-acid foods such as pickles, relishes, jams, compotes, and other fruit preserves. A hot water bath of 180°F to 190°F is reliable only for high-acid fruit juices and as a finishing step to other forms of processing, such as pickling. Pressure canning, a much-improved process, is necessary for canning low-acid foods.

Since you can use the process of canning for virtually everything from soup to nuts, it is definitely a versatile practice. Use canning for fruits, canned either raw or pre-cooked in a canning liquid, such as water, syrup, or juice. Use canning for vegetables, usually by the hot-pack method where they cook first, and then pack them in the cooking water. Process most vegetables in a pressure canner. The exceptions are pickles, relishes, and compotes made acidic by the addition of vinegar in the recipe.

There are vital steps to take before canning a batch of your home-grown produce. Make absolutely certain you do the following:

→ Use a *current* recipe and follow it precisely. Older recipes can be life-threatening.
→ Use only premium, perfectly ripe produce.
→ Use only new lids.
→ Wash each jar and check for any cracks or chips. Discard those with even the tiniest fractures.
→ Wash lids and rings; set in a pan, and cover with boiling water until ready to use.

For detailed instructions on canning, consult *Keeping the Harvest*, by Nancy Chioffi and Gretchen Mead (See "Recommended Reading List," page 157).

Freezing

A freezer is not a small investment. With the ease and certainty of food preservation a freezer provides, however, you might want to consider this major purchase.

The cost of freezers vary with upright models, chest types, and any special features offer. New models have an Energy Guide label, which details the cost of running them, which also varies.

 Tips for Low-Cost Freezer Operation

→ Don't position the freezer near a heat source, such as a furnace.

→ Make sure all freezer seals are tight; inspect the door gasket whenever adding to the freezer.

→ Keep the freezer set above 0°F.

→ Keep the freezer at least three-quarters full. Stock up on bread at the day-old store or fill empty spots in the freezer with ice-filled milk cartons or jugs.

→ Don't open the freezer door unless you must, then close it quickly!

Some fruits and vegetables freeze better than others. Some items, such as celery, turn to mush when thawed.

Pack fruits and freeze either in water, apple juice, or syrup. Dry-packed fruit is characteristically mushy when thawed. A syrup made by dissolving 1 to 3 cups of honey in 3 cups of boiling water not only sweetens, but also helps fruit maintain a firm texture. To freeze in liquid, pack the fruit into the container, then pour cooled liquid over the fruit to cover. Crumple up a piece of plastic wrap or wax paper, and place it over the fruit to keep it from bobbing up out of the liquid, which will discolor it.

Vegetables freeze best if blanched first. It helps them retain color, flavor, and texture. Many gardeners prefer steam blanching over boiling water, because the food retains more nutrients. Vegetables should be a uniform size, cut or chopped if necessary, so they blanch and freeze evenly. Immediately after blanching, plunge the vegetables into ice-water, or since soaking leaches nutrients, place them on a cookie sheet and pop into the freezer if you prefer. It takes roughly the same amount of time to properly cool food as it does to blanch it. Vegetables frozen without first undergoing this cooling stage turn out soggy. Finally, drain well before packing to prevent ice from forming in the containers.

The least expensive freezer containers are reusable ones, no matter what they cost initially. If handled carefully, this includes zip-seal freezer bags. Simply wash or rinse out, invert to dry, and store for the next season or crop.

If the unthinkable happens, and a power outage shatters the certainty of frozen foods, you still may be able to salvage frozen food. The basic rule of thumb is if ice-crystals are still present in the food, at the time you discover it or the power comes back on, and the temperature is 40°F or less, you can refreeze fruit, herbs, or vegetables. You will probably lose some quality, especially with vegetables, but the food is still safe to eat. You must toss completely thawed food that has been sitting out for an unknown amount of time. When in doubt, throw it out.

FRUITS AND VEGETABLES RECOMMENDED FOR FREEZING

FRUITS	VEGETABLES
Apples	Asparagus
Apricots	Beans, snap
Berries	Beans, lima
Cherries	Broccoli
Currants	Brussels
Grapes	sprouts
Melons — except	Carrots
watermelon	Cauliflower
Nectarines	Celeriac
Peaches	Corn
Strawberries	Greens
	Leeks
	Okra
	Peas, snap
	Peas, snow
	Peppers
	Squash
	Turnips

Pass It On

Homegrown, homemade garden gifts radiate a charm all their own. Prepare them for friends or family, or branch out and sell them. Remember one of the many fringe benefits of running your garden as a small business is the right to purchase all those items you would probably buy anyway at wholesale prices.

Say it With Flowers

Let the scent of the garden linger in the form of forced bulbs, bouquets, potpourris, or dried herb and flower wreaths. With this assortment, you can have gifts or merchandise from the garden year-round.

Forced bulbs are those manipulated into blooming out of season, usually in winter. You actually fool the bulbs rather than force them. To begin, place the bulbs in cold storage for about ten weeks. You can bag them in the refrigerator, or plant in pots and leave in a root cellar or cold frame. Cover smaller bulbs with soil mix, but leave larger types, such as hyacinth, daffodil, or tulips, with the growing tip exposed. Gradually move to warmer, lighter conditions as the bulbs sprout. Popular bulbs for forcing include fragrant hyacinths, crocus, daffodils, and other narcissus, amaryllis, and tulips.

Fresh-cut flowers are always in demand. A simple bouquet is an elegant gift, or ask a local merchant to sell your cut flowers. He may buy them outright, wholesale, or agree to sell them for you on consignment for a percentage.

Cut flowers in the morning, severing the stem at an angle to allow for maximum water intake. This helps keep the flowers fresh. Plunge immediately into cold water, and keep them there until you give or sell them. Flower preservatives help keep the bloom at its best, but a cheap substitute is a little non-diet lemon-lime soda. A clear or colored cellophane wrap, secured with a twist-tie, hidden by a bit of ribbon will protect bouquets bound for market.

Dried flower arrangements also are popular and will last indefinitely. Harvest flowers for drying just as the blossoms begin to open. Cut the flower stems as near to the ground as possible. Bind flowers together in bunches, and hang upside-down in a well-ventilated area out of direct sunlight to dry. When dry, arrange into bouquets, wrap the stems in a piece of colored tissue paper, and secure with a rubber band.

There are many recipes for potpourri, but it's easy to make with this simple formula:

1. **Pick fragrant blooms,** such as roses, hyacinth, lavender, jasmine, mock orange, or freesia, just before they open fully. Consider adding some blossoms that hold their color well when dried, such as calendula, borage, cornflowers, larkspur, statice, or strawflowers.
2. **Choose some scented leaves** from your herb bed, such as basil, lemon balm, lemon verbena, chamomile, mint, or sage.
3. **Air dry** the flowers and leaves on a cheesecloth frame, in a spot with good air circulation, out of direct sunlight.
4. **When dry, mix about 1 tablespoon of aromatic spices,** such as nutmeg, cinnamon, cloves, vanilla beans, ginger, or dried citrus peel, to every 4 cups of flowers and leaves.
5. **If desired, stir in a small amount of perfume fixative,** such as orris root, available at craft stores, and/or a few drops of essential oils, distilled fragrances available at drug stores.

There are two types of potpourri — moist and dry. The moist type is made with partially dried flowers and lasts for months. Keep in an airtight container and open occasionally to fill the room with its fragrance. Dry potpourri is a gift of the moment. Offer it in small jars or bowls salvaged from flea markets. Coat a styrofoam ball with glue and roll in the potpourri to coat. Sew some potpourri into sachets of fabric, lace, and ribbon, a great way to recycle a garage-sale dress!

▬ FLOWERS FOR FRESH OR DRIED ARRANGEMENTS ▬

FRESH-CUT FLOWERS	DRIED FLOWERS
Cosmos	Baby's breath
Columbine	Money plant
Sunflower	Statice
Dahlia	Strawflowers
Freesia	Ornamental
Gladiolus	grasses
Gloriosa	Rose buds
Iris	Yarrow
Lilies	
Daffodils	
Tulips	
Snapdragon	
Rose	
Ferns for greens	

While we are on the subject of dried flowers, consider giving or selling wreaths. Styrofoam forms, old wire coathangers, or straw forms, usually circle-shaped and bound with thread or fishing line, can all serve as forms for a garden wreath. Overlap dried flowers or herbs. Attach them with a hot glue gun or by tying flowers in place with thin wire, strong thread, or fishing line. Swags and garlands of greenery and flowers are attractive variations. Make wreaths from culinary herbs, medicinal herbs, single-color blossoms, fragrant blooms, or, for seasonal themes, holly, fall leaves, or fresh spring flowers.

Perchance a Purveyor of Plants

If you are already starting your own garden vegetables or flowers, consider going commercial. If you only have a few extra plants, offer them to your local garden center. Herbs and strawberry plants are always in demand. One-gallon tomato plants sell like hotcakes, and nobody seems to care if they grew in coffee cans. Remember that locally grown is a selling point! If you have grand designs, test the market with a roadside stand, or join your local farmers market or co-op. The best advice here is to try and beat the large producers to the market. If your product is available only a few days before the mass-produced kinds, it will sell first.

Share the Harvest

Whether you have an abundance of red, ripe tomatoes or a bumper crop of berries, homegrown food makes a great gift. Arrange a food basket and decorate the handle with some fresh or dried flowers. If baskets are scarce, make one by folding down the sides of a brown paper grocery bag, cutting vertical slits and weaving in horizontal strips cut from a second bag.

If you offer your produce at a roadside stand, consider consigning with other local gardeners or craftspeople to expand your merchandise and draw in more customers. Post signs down the road and again at the stand that stress locally grown, or pesticide free when appropriate.

Fruits and berries always seem to be more popular than broccoli and beets. Use them in recipes from muffins to flavored liqueurs for unique and tasteful gifts. Fruit-flavored spirits are easy to make. Place berries, cut peaches, or other fruit at the bottom of a jar, fill with vodka or brandy, and let steep for about two weeks. Strain, rebottle, and decorate for a special gift.

Don't forget the versatility of garden herbs. Give away or sell bunches of fresh culinary herbs, such as basil, parsley, or dill, or dry them and offer in decorated baby-food jars. Pack up some dried herbs, either culinary ones or those for soothing teas, and put in a gift basket. The dark glass jars yeast comes in are especially good for storing dried herbs. But I have never been able to part with them for gift-giving.

Herbal oils or vinegars are rare and appreciated treats to the gourmet. To make, fill a jar with slightly bruised, fresh herbs such as basil, garlic, mint, rosemary, tarragon, thyme, sage, lemon verbena, or even rose petals, and pour a light oil, such as safflower or sunflower oil, warmed cider, or wine vinegar over the herbs. Agitate every day for about two weeks, then taste. If not strong enough, repeat with a fresh batch of herbs. Collect glass salad dressing bottles with screw-on lids or odd bottles found at flea markets for containers; buy corks for stops. Wash thoroughly in hot, soapy water or boil to sterilize if you have any doubts. Place a sprig of the flavoring herb in the bottle for decorative effect and identification and fill with the oil or vinegar. For many more recipes for herbal vinegars, read *Herbal Vinegar* by Maggie Oster (see "Recommended Reading List," page 157).

Reserve these fun and thoughtful herbal gifts for your most intimate friends. Blend a special facial-steam potpourri to scatter into boiling water for a scented pore-opener. Or steep a scented massage oil, such as almond oil, grapeseed oil, hazelnut, or less expensive sesame seed oil for the base, with romantic rose petals, invigorating mint leaves, or your favorite scent or combination.

Finally, don't forget the many jam, jelly, pickle, relish, and other preserve recipes to make and give as gifts. Combine a few jars, add a sachet of potpourri, and a bottle of scented massage oil in a gift basket.

Make the most of your harvest by sharing it with others.

APPENDICES

APPENDIX A

COMPARATIVE TABLE
OF VEGETABLE PRODUCTION RATES

(per 10 foot of row)

PLANT	PLANTS/ 10 FT.	DAYS TO FIRST HARVEST	PRODUCTION/SQ. FT.	COST SAVINGS OF GROWING **
Asparagus*!!	10	2 years	5 – 8 pounds/Medium	High
Beans, bush!	35	55 – 75	6 – 8 pounds/High	Medium
Beans, pole!	35	65 – 90	10 – 12 pounds/High	Medium
Beets	50	65 – 80	10 – 12 pounds/High	Medium
Broccoli!	10	65 – 100	10 – 12 pounds/High	High
Brussels sprouts!!	10	100 – 120	15 pints/Low	High
Cabbage	8	60 – 90	10 – 15 pounds/Medium	Low
Cauliflower	9	50 – 75	8 – 10 pounds/Medium	High
Carrots!	60 – 80	65 – 90	12 pounds/High	Medium
Celery	20	100 – 120	20 stalks/Medium	Medium
Corn!!	20	65 – 120	40 ears/Medium	Medium
Cucumbers!	5	60 – 75	2 – 3 dozen/Low	High
Eggplant!!	5	80 – 100	15 – 20 pints/Low	High
Kohlrabi	30	50 – 75	7 – 8 pounds/Medium	Medium
Lettuce-leaf!	20	45 – 60	20 plants/Medium	High
Lettuce-head	8 – 10	75 – 80	8 – 10 heads/Low	Medium
Muskmelon	2	70 – 115	10 – 20 melons/Low	Medium
Muskmelon-trellised	10	70 – 115	50 – 80 melons/Medium	Medium
Onions-green!!	60 – 80	35 – 70	10 bunches/High	High
Onions-bulb	40	80 – 180	10 pounds/Medium	Low
Parsnips	40	110 – 150	10 – 15 pounds/Medium	Medium
Peas!!	60 – 100	45 – 120	10 – 12 pounds/Medium	Medium

Plant	Plants/ 10 ft.	Days to First Harvest	Production/Sq. Ft.	Cost Savings of Growing **
Peppers!	6	75 – 110	5 – 20 pounds/Low	High
Potatoes	10	80 – 140	20 pounds/Medium	Low
Pumpkins	3	95 – 110	10 pumpkins/Low	Low
Radishes	100 – 120	25 – 40	10 bunches/High	Medium
Rhubarb!*	3 – 4	2	15 – 20 pounds/High	High
Spinach!	30 – 40	45 – 60	5 pounds/Low	Medium
Squash-summer!!	3	55 – 70	25 pounds/High	High
Squash-winter	2	85 – 135	20 – 30 pounds/Medium	Low
Tomatoes!!	8	65 – 110	30 – 50 pounds/Medium	High
Turnips	30 – 40	60 – 70	20 pounds/High	Medium

Key: * Productive life of from 10 to 20+ years
   ** (compared to buying at store)
   ! Quality better than store-bought
   !! Quality *much* better than store-bought

(Compiled in part from Washington State Cooperative Extension Bulletin EB 0422)

APPENDIX B

HIGH-PRODUCTIVITY FRUIT VARIETIES

Fruit	Variety	Value	Years of Productivity
Blackberries (Combine varieties to extend harvest.)	1826, Chester, Hull, Arapaho, Silvan	High	10+
Blueberry (Must plant two cultivars for pollinations.)	Earliblue, Bluecrop*, Blueray, Northland**	High	50+
Currants** (Self-fertile)	Red Lake (red), Perfection (red), Magnus (black), Raven (black)	High	15 to 20+ 10
Elderberries	Native***	High	10+
Gooseberries** (Self-fertile)	Oregon Champion (green), Poorman (red), Pixwell (pink)	Medium	15 to 20+
Grapes (Table varieties)	Reliant (blush), Concord (purple), Catawba (red), Edelweiss (white), Moored (red)***, Niagara (green/ gold)	High	30+
Raspberries	Willamette (red), Sumner (red), 1836 (red), Heritage (fall-red), Munger Black Cap (black)	Medium	8 to 10
Strawberries			10+
Junebearing	Hood, Shuksan, Bentan		
Everbearing	Tillikum, Ogallalla		5+
Day Neutral	Tristar, Tribute		3

  * Drought resistant
 ** Good choice for northern gardeners
*** Disease resistant

APPENDIX C

Free (or at least cheap) Resources For Gardeners

Advice:
→ Cooperative Extension Service Office
The Cooperative Extension Service is organized by county. To find the office in your area, look in your phone book under "County Government." It may also be listed in regular listings as "Cooperative Extension Service." The staff is a great source of free advice on many gardening and food preparation and preservation topics. The Extension Service Office can give you phone numbers for the following programs in your area (or a nearby area if they are to be developed for your county):
→ Master Gardeners
→ Master Food Preservers
→ Master Composter
→ Master Food Preservers

Classes:
→ Master Gardeners
→ Master Composters
→ Master Food Preservers

Compost:
→ Community compost projects (Contact your local solid waste management agency for information on projects in your area. They may be listed in the phone book under city or town government. If you have trouble locating the right agency, call the county Cooperative Extension Service.

Help:
→ Community gardens
→ Urban gardening
→ Master Gardeners

Literature:
→ Local libraries (Many can request materials from other libraries as needed.)
→ Master Gardeners
→ County Extension Agents

→ State Land Grant Universities (Listed under "Schools" in your area Yellow Pages. Each state has a land grant university; they are the parent body of the Cooperative Extension Service. They offer published materials for a small fee, and you may also be able to access their library.)

→ Environmental Protection Agency (Listed under "Federal Government" in phone book.)

→ United States Department of Agriculture (Listed under "Federal Government" in phone book.)

Pesticides:

→ Hazardous Waste Drop-Off Site (Contact your local or state Department of Ecology hazardous waste management agency for information on disposal in your area.)

Pesticide Information:

→ National Pesticide Telecommunications Network (toll-free, 24 hour hotline) 1-800-858-7378, or FAX 806-743-3094

Seeds:

→ Master Gardeners (occasionally offered)

→ Seed Savers Exchange, Kent Whealy, Route 3, Box 239, Decovah, IA 52101

Speakers for Garden Clubs, Classes:

→ Master Gardeners

Trees:

→ Soil Conservation Service (Listed under "Federal Government" in phone book.)

APPENDIX D

Recommended Reading List

Bartholomew, Mel. *Square Foot Gardening*. Emmaus, Pennsylvania: Rodale Press, 1981. (Tells how to get the most from every square foot.)

Barton, Barbara. *Gardening By Mail: A Source Book*. Boston, Massachusetts: Houghton Mifflin Company, 1994.

Bubel, Nancy. *The New Seed-Starters Handbook*. Emmaus, Pennsylvania: Rodale Press, 1988. (Basics of starting from seed.)

Campbell, Stu. *Let It Rot! The Gardener's Guide to Composting*. Pownal, Vermont: Garden Way Publishing, 1990.

Campbell, Stu. *The Mulch Book: A Complete Guide for Gardeners*. Pownal, Vermont: Garden Way Publishing, 1991.

Chioffi, Nancy and Mead, Gretchen. *Keeping the Harvest*. Pownal, Vermont: Storey Communications, Inc., 1991. (Loaded with information on preserving what you grow.)

Davidson, Homer L. *Care and Repair of Lawn & Garden Tools*. Blue Ridge Summit, Pennsylvania: TAB Books, 1992. (Common sense advice on keeping your tools in working order.)

Denckla, Tanya. *The Organic Gardener's Home Reference: A Plant-by-Plant Guide to Growing Fresh, Healthy Food*. Pownal, Vermont: Garden Way Publishing, 1994.

Editors of Garden Way Publishing. *The Big Book of Gardening Skills*. Pownal, Vermont: Garden Way Publishing, 1993. (Comprehensive, illustrated guide to growing flowers, fruits, herbs, and vegetables, on a small or large scale. Numerous charts on planting, garden design, organic pest and disease control, succession planting, and more.)

Editors of Garden Way Publishing. *Just the Facts!* Pownal, Vermont: Garden Way Publishing, 1993. (Dozens of gardening charts.)

Ferguson, Nicola. *Right Plant, Right Place*. New York: Simon & Schuster, 1984. (Indispensable reference for landscaping.)

Foster, Catharine Osgood. *Building Healthy Gardens: A Safe and Natural Approach.* Pownal, Vermont: Garden Way Publishing, 1989. (The author presents new techniques and discoveries for reaping abundant harvests without chemical fertilizers, pesticides, or herbicides.)

Hart, Rhonda M. *Bugs, Slugs & Other Thugs.* Pownal, Vermont: Storey Communications, Inc., 1991. (Identifies pests and gives scores of non-toxic, often cheap, solutions.)

Hart, Rhonda M. *Trellising: How to Grow Climbing Vegetables, Fruits, Flowers, Vines, and Trees.* Pownal, Vermont: Storey Communications, Inc., 1992. (Includes how-to's on training fruit trees into double-duty hedges.)

Hill, Lewis. *Fruits and Berries For the Home Garden.* Pownal, Vermont: Garden Way Publishing, Storey Communications, Inc., 1977. (A good book on all aspects of fruit culture. Both entertaining and informative, Lewis goes the extra mile to explain the whys and hows behind so many orchard practices.)

Hill, Lewis. *Pruning Simplified, Updated Edition.* Pownal, Vermont: Garden Way Publishing, Storey Communications, Inc., 1986. (A great guide on how to prune everything from evergreens and ornamentals to fruit and nut trees. Useful illustrations of before-and-after proper pruning.)

Hill, Lewis. *Secrets of Plant Propagation: Starting Your Own Flowers, Fruits, Berries, Shrubs, Trees, and Houseplants.* Pownal, Vermont: Garden Way Publishing, 1985. (A complete guide to starting new plants.)

Hunt, Marjorie B. and Brenda Bortz. *High-Yield Gardening: How to get more from your garden space and more from your gardening season.* Emmaus, Pennsylvania: Rodale Press, 1986. (Chock full of useful suggestions for increasing your garden yield, this is a good general book for both beginning and experienced gardeners.)

Jacobs, Betty E.M. *Growing and Using Herbs Successfully.* Pownal, Vermont: Garden Way Publishing, 1981. (Complete information about herbs.)

Loewer, Peter. *Tough Plants For Tough Places.* Emmaus, Pennsylvania: Rodale Press, 1992. (Suggests a hundred surefire plants for challenging garden conditions.)

Marcin, Marietta Marshall. *The Herbal Tea Garden.* Pownal, Vermont: Garden Way Publishing, 1992.

McClure, Susan. *The Harvest Gardener.* Pownal, Vermont: Garden Way Publishing, 1992. (A compilation of tips and advice by the author and several other gardeners about choosing cultivars, scheduling plantings, organizing garden space, coping with the vagaries of weather and pests, harvesting and storing the crop. Also includes an encyclopedia of culture, harvest, and storage of fruits, herbs, and vegetables.)

Morgan, Hal. *The Mail Order Gardener.* New York: Harper & Row, Publishers, 1988. (Everything you might want to spend money on and more.)

Oster, Maggie. *Herbal Vinegar.* Pownal, Vermont: Storey Communications, 1994.

Pleasant, Barbara. *The Gardener's Bug Book: Earth-Safe Insect Control.* Pownal, Vermont: Storey Publishing, 1994.

Pleasant, Barbara. *The Gardener's Guide to Plant Diseases: Earth-Safe Remedies.* Pownal, Vermont: Storey Publishing, 1995.

Pleasant, Barbara. *Warm-Climate Gardening.* Pownal, Vermont: Garden Way Publishing, 1993. (The author offers advice about how to recognize and exploit the cool seasons within a warm-climate gardening year. Also includes information on drought-resistant plants, summer hardiness, and scheduling maintenance chores when it's too hot to garden.)

Powell, Eileen. *From Seed to Bloom: How to Grow Over 500 Annuals, Perennials, & Herbs.* Pownal, Vermont: Garden Way Publishing, 1995.

Raymond, Dick. *Down-to-Earth Gardening Know-How for the '90s: Vegetables and Herbs.* Pownal, Vermont: Storey Publishing, (revised and updated version), 1991. (A book full of useful charts and graph.)

Riotte, Louise. *Carrots Love Tomatoes: Secrets of Companion Planting for Successful Gardening.* Pownal, Vermont: Garden Way Publishing, 1975. (Vegetables and fruits have natural preferences; this book shows you how to arrange your garden to take advantage of these productive relationships.)

Riotte, Louise. *Roses Love Garlic: Secrets of Companion Planting With Flowers.* Pownal, Vermont: Garden Way Publishing, 1983. (The author explores companion planting with flowers and shows how to combine flower and vegetable gardens for a striking display of color, form, and productivity.)

Riotte, Louise. *Successful Small Food Gardens: Vegetables, Herbs, Flowers, Fruits, Nuts, Berries.* Pownal, Vermont: Garden Way Publishing, 1993. (This newly revised and updated edition of Riotte's classic intensive-gardening book addresses the needs of the small-space garden. Included is information on companion plants, succession planting, raised beds, container growing, watering and drainage, increasing soil quality, edible flowers, herbs, and shrubs.)

Rogers, Marc. *Saving Seeds: The Gardener's Guide to Growing and Storing Vegetable and Flower Seeds.* Pownal, Vermont: Storey Publishing, 1990. (A small paperback, this is an easy guidebook to saving seeds. It presents general principles and specifics for each vegetable.)

Schwenke, Karl and Sue. *Build Your Own Stone House Using the Easy Slipform Method.* Pownal, Vermont: Storey Communications, Inc, 1975, 1991. (Gives complete instructions on how to build rock walls for raised beds, retaining walls, coldframes and more.)

Whealy, Kent, ed. *The Garden Seed Inventory.* Decorah, Iowa: Seed Saver Publishing, 1992. (As the Director of the Seed Savers Exchange, Whealy compiles a complete listing of all [over 5,000] nonhybrid varieties offered by over 200 seed companies. Each entry describes the variety, provides synonyms, provides a range of maturity dates and lists all known sources. Known by some as the seed savers' bible.)

Whitner, Jan Kowalczewski. *Stonescaping.* Pownal, Vermont: Storey Communications, Inc. 1992. (Ideas and directions for using stone, including step-by-step instructions for making hypertufa [stonelike cement-mix] planters, birdbaths, etc.)

Yeomans, Kathleen, RN. *The Able Gardener.* Pownal, Vermont: Garden Way Publishing, 1992. (Tips, techniques, and inspiration to make gardening easier and more enjoyable no matter what your ability. Included are practical techniques like raised beds and automatic watering systems, and imaginative suggestions like fragrance and indoor gardens.)

INDEX

Page references in *italic* indicate illustrations.

DISCARDED

8|03